i still love you

ive plays by
Daniel MacIvor

I Still Love You

five plays by
Daniel MacIvor

Never Swim Alone

The Soldier Dreams

You Are Here

In On It

A Beautiful View

Playwrights Canada Press
Toronto • Canada

PLAYWRIGHTS CANADA PRESS
The Canadian Drama Publisher
215 Spadina Ave., Suite 230, Toronto, Ontario, Canada, M5T 2C7
phone 416.703.0013   fax 416.408.3402
orders@playwrightscanada.com • www.playwrightscanada.com

For professional production rights contact Thomas Pearson, International Creative Management
(ICM) 825 Eighth Avenue, New York, NY 10019
212-556-6656   fax 212-556-5794   tpearson@icmtalent.com
For amateur rights and further information contact   danielmacivor.com

The publisher acknowledges the support of the Canadian taxpayers through the Government of Canada Book Publishing Industry Development Program, the Canada Council for the Arts, the Ontario Arts Council, and the Ontario Media Development Corporation.

Cover photo: Daniel MacIvor. Cover design: JLArt
Production editor: MZK

Library and Archives Canada Cataloguing in Publication

MacIvor, Daniel, 1962-
I still love you : five plays / by Daniel MacIvor.

Contents: Never swim alone -- The soldier dreams -- You are here -- In on it -- A beautiful view
ISBN 978-0-88754-858-1

I. Title.

PS8575.I86I5 2006   C812'.54   C2006-902614-9

First edition: July 2006. Third printing: May 2009.
Printed and bound by AGMV Marquis at Quebec, Canada.

Every best effort was made by the publisher to locate the following people for permission to use photographs which appear in this book. Anyone knowing their whereabouts, please ask them to contact Playwrights Canada Press or advise the Press as to where they might be contacted.
They are:

Photographers:	Jacques Oulé (*The Soldier Dreams*)
	Kevin Fitzsimons (*A Beautiful View*)
	Dona Ann McAdams (*In On It*)
Actor:	Volker Burger (*The Soldier Dreams*)

• Table of Contents •

• Preface: "The End is the Beginning" •

The plays in this collection were developed and first presented by da da kamera, a company I formed in 1986 and first tried to close in 1991.

In 1986 I was just out of George Brown College in Toronto and was trying to make new work together with a group of friends including Michelle Jelley, James Cameron, Caroline Gillis, Corey Reay and Lisa Lelliott. We were a collection of many-hatted actors, directors, designers, video artists and playwrights. We were making work in places like the back room of the Rivoli on Queen Street West and at the celebrated Buddies In Bad Times Rhubarb! Festival. After about a year that group had dwindled to Caroline Gillis, myself, and my then boyfriend Albert Chevalier. Together we didn't really know what we were doing other than we wanted to make theatre that was engaging and alive and that we wanted to travel with the work. I wrote a one-woman play for Caroline called *See Bob Run*. Albert thought it was the best play he had ever read—though he hadn't read many plays. I think what struck him most was the power of Bob's voice, and the spirit in which the play was written: quickly, desperately and lovingly. I had written the play for Caroline because I wanted her to have a career and be happy, I guess I also wrote the play for Albert because I wanted him to have a project to work on, and I wrote it for myself in order to bring us all closer together. We were living in an apartment on Berkeley Street in Cabbagetown and always struggling to make the rent. Albert was sure that *See Bob Run* was going to be our ticket to success. It was our lack of knowledge about the way things worked that allowed us to be convinced by Albert to approach the best director we had seen and offer him the play of an unknown playwright with an unknown actress and unknown producer attached. That director, Ken McDougall, was intrigued by this curious group of friends and something in the play interested him. Ken was a close friend of Sky Gilbert, Buddies In Bad Times' Artistic Director, and Sky, never one to be afraid of oddballs and outcasts, came up with some seed money for the show and co-produced with us at The Poor Alex Theatre. The show was something of a small sensation and although we didn't really make any money we had our first taste of creative success. Somewhere along the way we picked up stage manager Claudine Domingue and bolstered by our Toronto experience launched da da kamera's first national tour, produced by Albert and his credit cards. We took the play to Victoria, Vancouver, Edmonton, Montreal and Halifax. Something was beginning.

It was now the late 80s and I began to create new work with Ken and Toronto playwright/actor/director Edward Roy. Together in various combinations we made *Never Swim Alone, 2-2-Tango, Yes I Am And Who Are*

You?, *This Is A Play*, *White Trash Blue Eyes*, and *Theatre Omaha's Production of The Sound of Music* to name a few. We all had our own companies—I was da da kamera, Ken (with Robin Fulford) was Platform 9 and Edward was Topological Theatre—indeed it appeared at that time that everyone had their own theatre company. It seemed to me that each of those companies was really just a pseudonym for the artist or artists making the work—I didn't think about aesthetic or mandate—a mandate was just something I had to write for an art council grant. All I knew was that I wanted to make work that excited me and that gave me a sense of belonging. With the help of people like Sky at Buddies, Deanne Taylor at Video Cabaret and Sara Muerling at the Theatre Centre, da da kamera had gained a reputation for doing interesting work and so our Theatre Centre production of *Never Swim Alone* had a restaging at Theatre Passe Muraille. This was a big deal. The show was a success but the world was changing, AIDS was devastating our community, and people were asking a lot of questions about why we were doing this work. Albert had died. Others were ailing. Then Ken got sick. Something was ending.

At the opening night party for *Never Swim Alone* the woman who worked as the publicist at Passe Muraille was standing near me at the bar and overheard me tell a friend that I was going to close da da kamera. I was overwhelmed with the paperwork, it was over, kaput. The publicist approached me and she said "If you stop doing theatre I'm stopping too." This woman was Sherrie Johnson. I didn't know Sherrie very well but I knew she was devoted to theatre. She had been working part-time with Toronto madman/genius Hillar Liitoja's DNA Theatre and at Passe Muraille she had spearheaded a publicity campaign for *Never Swim Alone* which saw subway ads, a first for Toronto theatre. Also, she was always hanging around the theatre while we were working, looking for any excuse to watch the process, apparently she almost lost her job because "the theatre is no place for the publicist" (and we wonder why we have problems with the system?). The thing I had discovered about Sherrie was that although she didn't actually write or act or direct she was an artist. A couple of days later Sherrie came to my apartment on Maitland Street and we talked about how we could do something together. We wanted to make work that was engaging and alive and we wanted the work to travel, other than that we had no idea what we were doing. Something was beginning.

Around that time I had begun a creative partnership with the Toronto director/playwright Daniel Brooks—who ran The Augusta Company with Tracy Wright and Don McKellar. Brooks and I were playing with notions of theme and style and together we had made the solo show *House* which, with the help of producer Colin Rose, we had toured to Israel, Glasgow and Manchester. More recently we had been examining the life and work of the playwright Federico Garcia Lorca and taken a three-week trip to Spain which resulted in the creation of *The Lorca Play*. Sherrie managed to bring *The Lorca Play* to the attention of Marie-Helene Falcon from Montreal's Festival des Ameriques and the play was offered an invitation to the festival. This was really the first time the company's work was seen at a festival where presenters from other festivals come looking for work to program, and although *The Lorca Play* was too unwieldy for a young company to tour— with eight actors and a four-person design team—we saw what was possible.

The following years saw Sherrie and Brooks and I as a team making *Here Lies Henry*, *The Soldier Dreams* and *Monster*, among other shows. We each had our role: Sherrie was producing, Brooks was directing, and I was writing and performing, but more than that we had a profound love for one another and the shared energy of a desire to make work that was more than just a "good job done" and to make a life that was entwined with our work. It was around the time of *Monster* that Brooks was considering becoming an official partner of the company. It was Brooks who helped me to believe that my ideas were important, who showed me that my self was worth celebrating and examining, and allowed me my artistic vision. Much of the work he had done on the solo shows helped to define da da kamera's visual style. He was an essential part of the work we were doing. But I was hungry to direct. When Brooks and I were working together on larger projects we would always fall into our familiar roles: he the director, me the playwright. I was worried that with Brooks as a partner I would never develop as a director. I told him I didn't want him to become a full partner. It was very difficult for me, but I imagine more so for him. It was not an easy time but it is a testament to our love for one another that our friendship remains strong and committed and we continue to work together.

It was the following years that produced the work *You Are Here* and *In On It*. Sherrie had managed to build da da kamera up into one of the most successful international touring companies in the country. The work had been seen throughout the US and UK, in Israel again, the Czech Republic, in Australia at the amazing Sydney Opera House, in Norway, Ireland and all across Canada from the tiny Festival Antigonish in Nova Scotia to the National Arts Centre in Ottawa, we had forged ongoing and important developmental partnerships with Chuck Helm at the Wexner Center at Ohio State University, with Mark Russell at New York's P.S. 122 and Danièle de Fontenay at Montreal's Usine C. *You Are Here* had played in sold-out runs in Toronto and Halifax and *In On It* toured more than any of our other shows and had won an Obie Award in New York. Sherrie had become one of the best international producers in the country and da da kamera needed more months in the year to attempt to visit all the cities to which we had invitations. Around this time we began work on the solo show *Cul-de-sac* for the Festival du monde in Montreal with Brooks directing, it was a deeply difficult process (as Brooks so brilliantly and succinctly outlines in his forward to the published script) but the show was clearly one of our best. A long road of touring stretched out before us. But I was growing tired. I was turning 40 and spending up to eight months of the year on the road. I remembered how when we had first talked about the company Sherrie had said she would rather not handle the finances and now here she was besieged with spreadsheets and accountants and corporate gobbledygook. Not only that, Sherrie and I had begun to develop and produce film together and she was running Six Stages, her own international theatre festival. Sherrie was trapped in the office and I was trapped on the road. In order to escape I moved from Toronto to Halifax in an attempt to slow my life down, but because of touring I spent little time in Halifax. I needed a break, but I didn't know how to stay still, so I took two months off to drive through the deserts of the American Southwest. It was in New Mexico that I remember feeling resentment about da da kamera and how much they expected of me. I suddenly realized, I was "them." I e-mailed Sherrie and told her that I had to stop working this way. When I received her reply I was moved to tears, she felt the same way. Something was ending.

Sherrie never met Albert. I wish she could have. They are certainly kindred spirits. And I would never say that Sherrie picked up from where Albert left off, Sherrie is far too much her own person with her own creative fuel to be described that way. But together they would have been an unstoppable team. Of course as I write those words I realize that is what Sherrie and I became. Until we decided to stop, to change. Without question both Sherrie and I will continue to make theatre, but not this way. Not the way da da kamera made theatre: where all artists are present in the process from the beginning of the idea, where each element of production is of equal and essential value, and where development continues years into the life of the production. Companies are too concerned with the bottom line for that, here in this world where theatre is produced like it's real estate and the people who sell the work exist in a world far, far away from the creation of the work. But of course you might change all that.

Something has ended. And that is a good thing. I am happy to have had this time, to have loved these people, to have done this work. And in the end I have learned that meaning is revealed in retrospect, that aesthetic is developed not intended, and that absence is required for depth to be discovered. The plays in this collection came from da da kamera, and if any one thing, these plays are about how we must welcome death and embrace endings in order to move forward, even to begin. As we entered the final stages of development for *A Beautiful View* we were aware that it would be the last new creation of da da kamera. The process leading up to the world premiere at the Wexner Center was a wonderful and calm time. Charmed even. And knowing it was the last show certainly effected what the play became: a story which closes with two people sitting at the end of the world looking at one another and seeing in each other their best selves. We couldn't hope for a more perfect final image.

Daniel MacIvor
Guysborough, Nova Scotia
March, 2006

• Foreword: "Dancing With MacIvor" •

My relationship to the plays of Daniel MacIvor has been as producer, director, audience member and most recently, as teacher. I am not alone in admiring his unstoppable artistic output and in being astonished again and again by realizing that what seems simple is suddenly complex in the best possible way. This happens in both his writing and his production style—that is—the way he "makes" a play. Each play adds up to a theatre experience which is so intriguing that we find ourselves going back through our memory of watching it, or re-reading the play to note exactly how and at what point every detail, every word was laid in. Often in MacIvor's plays, and in the five plays in this collection, we, the audience, are acknowledged— we are not on the other side of the fourth wall. Our presence is part of the experience we are all going through together in the same room, but that experience is not always comfortable, and it doesn't stop the imaginary world of the play from gaining power and grabbing us by the throat.

That is what happened to me in early 2001 when I saw the play, *In On It*, at the Belfry theatre in Victoria. *In On It* has a disarming simplicity. We are introduced to the several characters performed by two men with minimal props—two chairs, a grey sports jacket, a tissue and set of keys. Gradually, we are let "in on it." Tiny details of each character's circumstances are exchanged so casually that we are carried along by the overlapping stories blissfully unaware of the final catastrophe. Early in *In On It*, Brian, speaking to the audience says: "There are the things that happen out of careful planning— and then there are the things that sneak up on us—the things that happen over which we have no control." It is breathtaking how this play suddenly takes on the tragic force of the inevitable. The play captures the poignancy of ordinary lives suddenly turned upside down by the unexpected. MacIvor identifies the main theme of *In On It* as "grief." Touring to New York just after the 9/11 attacks this play became a magnet for New Yorkers and later that year Daniel MacIvor was presented with an Obie for *In On It*.

I find a strong thematic relationship between *In On It* and his next most recent play in this collection—*The Soldier Dreams*. While attending a workshop production of *The Soldier Dreams* at Buddies In Bad Times in Toronto, I was struck by MacIvor's exploration of how "choice" and "chance" together determine our destiny. Were it not for one or the other everything would turn out differently. In this play, we learn details about David through the stories told by family and friends who are in vigil at his bedside. Threaded through this scene are the past events revealed by "memory David" who is present to us, but unseen by the others. He shows us how, while visiting Ottawa to be best man at a planned event—his sister's wedding—he chanced to meet a student from Germany, and through the choices that followed their meeting, David arrived at the place where he is at this moment—dying with AIDS. The combination of mere chance and those choices lead to his untimely death.

MacIvor's fine ear for the female voice impressed me deeply when I had the opportunity to direct his play, *Marion Bridge* in 2003. Later at McGill, while teaching "monologue, storytelling and direct address" in his plays—the students found and explored many of these female voices—some of which had only been performed by him. This exploration of MacIvor's women characters coincided with an opportunity to see the newest play in this collection—*A Beautiful View* in a workshop presentation at Usine C in Montreal, with Tracy Wright and Caroline Gillis. MacIvor again uses direct address to have both women wryly reveal truths about themselves to us, while showing a completely different face to the other character. We become complicit in their roller-coaster relationship which is based on misconceptions—each believing the other to be a lesbian and herself to be heterosexual. Their evasions and confusions lead to lots of laughter. However, time and fraught circumstances ultimately bring this unlikely pair together—in fact they face death together, and—again it sneaks up on us—we discover they have actually been telling us the story of their lives from the other side. In *A Beautiful View*, mortality is once more a vital ingredient which lends an amazing perspective and depth to the work.

This conceit of telling the story from the other side is used in another play which is included in this collection—*You Are Here*—the story of Alison, as told by Alison. The bottle of sand from a desert near the Dead Sea which she shows to us at the beginning of the play resonates with time and mortality. Throughout the play, we await its reappearance with apprehension. Midway through the second act Alison turns to the audience and says: "Retrospect is everything…. It is the road ahead of you and the horizon behind you. In retrospect it all comes together. All the little details turn into that road map you didn't know you'd been following all this time. All this long time. And in retrospect we look back to see how we got there. What it must have been that got us there, how it must have happened." Throughout the play, Alison reveals various events and relationships, and ultimately the hidden tragedy in the story—her "too late" realization about her only real love. Very simply, it's given to us in the final scene of the play, after all the sand has run out of the bottle. And then we find ourselves in the same position as Alison—looking back over her life—with "retrospect."

Never Swim Alone, first presented in 1991 at the Tarragon Theatre in Toronto is the earliest of the MacIvor plays in this publication—and because it's a play about competition between men, the play itself is set up like a competition. The referee is played by a woman who keeps score and determines who wins each round. Late in the play, Frank says to the audience "The winner has, and will always, rule… being first, my friends is the point."

The sad truth is that what really binds these two established men is a different point—the point to which they were racing many years before, when a young girl drowned because they wouldn't stop to help her for fear of losing the race. In spite of the nagging, eroding memory of this shared secret, the referee—who is also the young girl, brings them face to face in a last deadly round. Having set them up in this final irresistible drive for the prize, she exits. Even in this very early play—when this simple dramatic metaphor concludes, it leaves us in a deeper place—thinking about men and games of power and the world around us.

The five plays in this collection span 15 years of writing from 1991–2006 and each successive play has greater depth and offers greater themes and perspectives. While each tale has a tragedy within it, Daniel MacIvor's writing retains a unique charm, a lively playfulness, sometimes with dancing, and plenty of humour. The exploration of the ironies of "the human condition"—is what makes MacIvor's work so fascinating. He tells a good story, but he has something well beyond the story to say, and it has that ring of being about us.

Linda Moore,
Montreal
March, 2006

The plays in this collection are dedicated to

Albert Chevalier
and
Sherrie Johnson

Never Swim Alone

l to r: Steve Cumyn, Sigrid Johnson, Daniel MacIvor
photo by Guntar Kravis

Never Swim Alone was first produced by da da kamera and Platform 9 Theatre at the Theatre Centre, Queen Street West, Toronto, in February 1991, with the following company:

REFEREE . . . . Caroline Gillis
A. FRANCIS DELORENZO . . . . Robert Dodds
WILLIAM (BILL) WADE . . . . . . Daniel MacIvor

Directed by Ken McDougall
Designed by Steve Lucas
Stage Managed by Anne Driscoll

•

Never Swim Alone was later produced with a cast change at Theatre Passe Muraille with the following:

REFEREE . . . . Sigrid Johnson
A. FRANCIS DELORENZO . . . . Steve Cumyn
WILLIAM (BILL) WADE . . . . . . Daniel MacIvor

Characters

REFEREE
FRANK
BILL

Never Swim Alone

*On stage: Up centre a tall referee chair, stage left a small table
and chair for BILL, stage left a small table and chair for FRANK.
A scoreboard. As the audience enters the woman lies on stage under
a sheet. Nostalgic summer beach music playing.*

*FRANK, a man in a blue suit, and BILL, an almost imperceptibly
shorter man in a blue suit, enter through the house greeting the
audience, singling people out: "Hey glad you could come." "Nice to
see you again." "That's a great shirt." "Call me Friday." etc. They
step on stage and turn to the audience.*

FRANK & BILL   *(in unison)* Hello.
Good to see you.
Glad you could come.

> *They slowly lift the sheet from the REFEREE. She rises, she wears
> a blue bathing suit, she looks out and steps down centre.*

REFEREE   A beach.
A bay.
The point.
Two boys on a beach. Late afternoon. They have been here all day, and
they have been here all day every day all summer. It is the last day of
summer before school begins. Nearby is a girl. She as well has been
here all day, and all day every day all summer. She lies on her green
beach towel in her blue bathing suit with her yellow radio. The boys
have been watching the girl from a distance all summer, but now that
the summer is nearly over, the boys are braver and watch from very
close by. She reminds one boy of his sister, she reminds the other of
a picture of a woman he once saw in a magazine. She thinks the boys
are funny. She thinks the boys are cute. She turns her head a little over
her shoulder and speaks to the boys: "Race you to the point?"

This is the beach.
Here is the bay.
There is the point.

> *The REFEREE steps to her chair and takes her place. She blows her
> whistle. The men exit.*

Round One: "Stature."

> *The REFEREE blows her whistle to begin Round One.
> We hear footsteps.*

FRANK & BILL   (*offstage*) Two. Two. Two. Two. Two. Two. Two. Two. Men enter a room.

>   *FRANK and BILL enter.*

FRANK   Good to see you.

BILL   Good to see you Frank.

FRANK   How long's it been?

BILL   Weeks?

FRANK   Months?

BILL   Too long Frank.

FRANK   Too long indeed Bill.

FRANK & BILL   How's things?
Can't complain.
How's the family?
Just great.
How's business?
Well a whole heck of a lot better than it was this time last year let me tell you.
Ha ha ha.
How's the blood pressure.
(*aside and snide*) Ha ha ha.

FRANK   Two men.

BILL   Two men.

FRANK & BILL   Two men enter a room. A taller man and—

>   *They stop. They laugh. As they speak they each gesture that he is the taller man.*

A taller man and—
A taller man and—
A taller man and—
A taller man and—

>   *REFEREE ends the round. The men stand side by side facing her. She inspects them carefully, measuring their height. She gives the victory to FRANK. BILL takes his seat. FRANK steps front and centre addresses the audience.*

FRANK   A. Francis DeLorenzo. My friends call me Frank. The "A" is for Alphonse and not even my enemies call me Alphonse. Alphonse Francis DeLorenzo: French, English, Italian. Behold before you a square of the Canadian quilt. To those of you I didn't have a chance to greet as

I entered I'd like to welcome you and thank you for coming. I'm sure you all have busy schedules and many other concerns in these troubled times and your presence here tonight is greatly appreciated. A hand for the audience! And if I might I would like to start off with a favourite quote of mine: "We do not place especial value on the possession of virtue until we notice its total absence in our opponent." Friedrich Nietzsche. Once again, thanks for coming.

> *FRANK resumes his seat.*

REFEREE   Round Two: "Uniform."

> *REFEREE blows her whistle to begin Round Two.*

FRANK & BILL   Two men enter a room.

FRANK   A taller man and

BILL   an almost imperceptibly shorter man.

FRANK   They both wear

FRANK & BILL   White shirts. Blue suits. Silk ties. Black shoes. Black socks. White shirts, blue suits, silk ties, black shoes, black socks. White shirts blue suits silk ties black shoes black socks. Whiteshirts bluesuits silkties blackshoes blacksocks. Whiteshirtsbluesuitssilktiesblackshoesblacksockswhiteshirtsbluesuit-ssilktiesblackshoesblacksocks. White shirts:

BILL   A hundred and fifty at Harry Rosen.

FRANK & BILL   Blue suits:

FRANK   Nine twenty two twenty two

BILL   on sale

FRANK   at Brogue.

FRANK & BILL   Silk ties:

BILL   came with the suit?

FRANK   Present.

BILL   From Donna?

FRANK   Ah… no.

BILL   Oh. It's nice.

FRANK   How's Sally.

BILL   Oh good good. How's Donna?

FRANK   Oh good good.

BILL   How's the house?

FRANK   Very good.

FRANK & BILL   How's the boy?
Just fine.
Now there's an investment eh?

FRANK   Three?

BILL   Four?
Five?

FRANK   Four.

FRANK & BILL   Right right.
Good kid?
Great kid.
Smart kid?
A little genius.
Must get it from his mother.
Ha ha ha ha ha ha ha.
Black shoes:

FRANK   Two twenty five even, David's Uptown.

FRANK & BILL   Black socks:

BILL   *(excitedly noting FRANK's socks) Blue socks!*

> *REFEREE ends the round. She inspects the men's socks. She gives the victory to BILL. FRANK takes his seat. BILL steps out and addresses the audience.*

Hello to all the familiar faces in the audience tonight and a very extra hello to all the friends I haven't met yet. William (Bill) Wade: Canadian, Canadian, Canadian. That's what's beautiful about this country: doesn't matter where you come from once you're here you're a Canadian, and that makes me proud. And I'd also like to add a bit of a quote myself, as my old man always used to say: "If bullshit had a brain it would quote Nietzsche." Thank you.

> *BILL resumes his seat.*

REFEREE   Round Three: "Who Falls Dead The Best."

> *REFEREE begins Round Three.*

FRANK & BILL   Two men enter a room.

BILL   And each man carries—

FRANK & BILL   —a briefcase.

FRANK   The first man seems very much like the second man and—

BILL   —the first man seems very much like the second man.

FRANK & BILL   Yes.

FRANK   But—

BILL   —they—

FRANK   —are—

FRANK & BILL   —not.

FRANK   For two reasons.

BILL   Two.

FRANK   One:

FRANK & BILL   one man is the first man and,

BILL   two:

FRANK & BILL   one man, in his briefcase has—

REFEREE   A gun.

FRANK   A gun.

BILL   A gun.

FRANK & BILL   A gun.

BILL   Which man is—

FRANK   —the first man and—

BILL   —which man has—

FRANK & BILL   —the gun?

> *FRANK and BILL mime shooting one another in slow motion. They die elaborately also in slow motion. REFEREE ends the round. The men face the REFEREE. She calls a tie. FRANK and BILL step forward and address the audience.*

I've known this guy for years.

BILL   Years.

FRANK   And this is sad—

FRANK & BILL   —but it's true...

BILL   And when I say years—

FRANK   —I mean years.

FRANK & BILL   I mean—

FRANK   —I saw the look of another woman in his father's eyes.

BILL   I smelled the bourbon on his mother's breath.

FRANK   I kept it a secret his aunt was his sister.

BILL   I knew his brother was gay before he did.

FRANK & BILL   I mean years.

FRANK   I mean—

BILL   —we spent summers together.

FRANK & BILL   Real summers—

BILL   —when you're a kid.

FRANK   Remember real summers—

FRANK & BILL   —when you were a kid?

FRANK   It stayed bright till nine o'clock and when it did get dark it got so dark you never wanted to go home.

BILL   Smoking roll-your-owns in the woods with a *Playboy* magazine and warm beer from somebody's father's basement.

FRANK & BILL   No school and Kool-Aid, and baseball and hide and seek late at night and hot dogs and full moons and overnights outside and swimming.

FRANK   And when they said not to swim alone—

BILL   —this—

FRANK   —here—

FRANK & BILL   —this is the guy I swam with!

BILL   I know this guy better than he knows himself.

FRANK   And that's what makes it sad—

BILL   —but sad as it is it's true—

FRANK & BILL   —and the truth of it is:

FRANK   And this is much—

BILL   —much—

FRANK & BILL   —much more—

FRANK   —than something as simple as—

BILL   —his bad nerves—

FRANK   —his trouble sleeping—

BILL   —his shaky marriage—

FRANK   —his failing business—

BILL   —his dizzy spells—

FRANK   —his bad check ups—

BILL   —his spotty lungs—

FRANK   —his heart—

FRANK & BILL   —pa pa pa pa pa pa pa pa pa pa palpitations—

FRANK   —this is—

BILL   —much—

FRANK   —much—

FRANK & BILL   —much sadder than that.

FRANK   He's not happy.

FRANK & BILL   He's not happy at all.

BILL   He feels cornered.

FRANK   He feels stuck.

BILL   He feels tied.

FRANK   He feels bound.

FRANK & BILL   He feels trapped.

BILL   And he's a relatively

FRANK   still a relatively young man.

BILL   And I'm just saying that—

FRANK   —for a relatively young man—

FRANK & BILL   —that's really sad.

>   *FRANK and BILL resume their seats.*

REFEREE   Round Four: "Friendly Advice Part One."

>   *FRANK and BILL bring their chairs centre and sit. REFEREE begins Round Four.*

BILL   Okay here's the story, these are the facts, this is where I stand, this is the point from which I view the situation.

FRANK   Go on.

BILL   Your situation.

FRANK   Yes.

BILL   I'm not going to pull any punches, I'm not going to cut any corners. I'm not going to give you the short shrift, I'm not going to shovel the shit.

FRANK   The only way to be.

BILL   The only way to be.

FRANK & BILL   Straight up!

BILL   Can I get personal?

FRANK   Personal?

BILL   We're friends.

FRANK   And?

BILL   Well Frank… I've got two good eyes I can't help but see, I've got two good ears I can't help but hear what's being said, and what's being said, around, is… Frank, I'm not saying I've got the goods on what makes a marriage work, God knows me and Sally, the honeymoon was over long ago but Frank… it works! And maybe that's just communication and maybe that's just luck but Frank…. All I'm trying to say here buddy is if you ever need an outside eye, if you ever need a friendly ear, then hey, I'm here.

FRANK   Are you thinner?

BILL   What?

FRANK   Are you thinner?

BILL   No.

FRANK   You're not thinner?

BILL   No I'm just the same.

FRANK   Really?

BILL   Same as always.

FRANK   It must just be your hair.

> *REFEREE ends the round. She calls the men forward. She looks at the top of BILL's head. She gives the victory to FRANK. BILL takes his seat. FRANK steps forward.*

Last Saturday night I'm on the street after before-dinner cocktails on my way uptown. I flag a cab, I tell him where I'm going, he says. "Okay." All right. Driving light cars thinking so on, and he says something about the night and I say something about the moon and he says something about the weather and I say "Yeah."
The radio on and I say something about the music and he says

something about the singer and we both say "Yeah."
All right. Driving lights cars thinking so on.
Now; on the radio a commercial. "Butter Butter Eat Butter" or
something. "Milk Milk Drink Milk" or whatever and he says something
about cows and I say something about horses and he says: "Do you
like horses?" and I think about it… and I think about it and I realize….
Dammit yes! Yes I do! I have never thought about it before but I am the
kind of guy who likes horses. The kind of guy who likes John Wayne
and Wild Turkey and carpentry and fishing on lazy August afternoons
and horses. Then he says something about the moon and I say
something about the night. But you see… I like horses.
Thank you.

> *FRANK resumes his seat.*

BILL   You're a real cowboy.

> *REFEREE calls a foul on BILL.*

REFEREE   Round Five: "Friendly Advice Part Two."

> *FRANK and BILL bring their chairs centre and sit. REFEREE begins
> Round Five.*

FRANK   Seen Phil lately?

BILL   Oh yeah sure.

FRANK   Phil's a good guy, eh?

BILL   The best.

FRANK   The best yes. The kind of guy a guy admires. A guy who's
got it all together. A guy who picks his friends carefully because he
understands a friend is a mirror; a reflection of the thing before it.

BILL   So.

FRANK   I mean… look, I'm not going to pull any punches and I don't
want you to take this the wrong way but Phil mentioned it and Phil
knows we're tight and I'm sure he wouldn't have mentioned it to me
if he didn't think I would mention it to you. I mean he likes you. I'm
almost sure he does. He thinks you're a fine guy, a good guy, he does,
but he mentioned that maybe lately you… and I don't… I'm only
saying this out of concern, as I'm sure Phil was as well… but he
mentioned that, maybe lately, you've been a little on the—well…
a bit—how did he put it? A bit too "palpably desperate" I think was
his phrase. And Bill you can't hold yourself responsible for the fact
that business is bad, it's not your fault and tomorrow's another day
no matter how bad things seem right now. And Phil is worried he
wouldn't have mentioned it otherwise, and hey, I'm worried too. And

I think you should be complimented…. You should take it as a compliment to your character that a good guy like Phil is concerned about you.

BILL   That's funny.

FRANK   Funny?

BILL   Yeah. He didn't mention it last night.

FRANK   Last night?

BILL   We saw a movie.

> *REFEREE moves to end the round. FRANK stops her.*

FRANK   Which movie?

BILL   "High Noon."

FRANK   What time?

BILL   Seven-forty.

FRANK   We're going to the game on Thursday.

BILL   We're going to Montreal for the weekend.

FRANK   We're driving to Arizona for Christmas.

BILL   I'm taking his son camping.

FRANK   He asked me to lend him fifty bucks.

BILL   He wants me to help him build his house.

FRANK   He asked me to be his executor.

BILL   His wife made a pass at me.

FRANK   That dog?

> *REFEREE stops the round. She gives the victory to BILL. FRANK takes his seat. BILL steps forward.*

BILL   Not only do I like horses, I love horses, I have ridden horses, I have ridden horses bareback, I have owned a horse, I have seen my horse break its leg and I have shot my horse. And not only have I shot my horse I have made love in a stable.

> *BILL resumes his seat.*

FRANK   With whom, the horse?

> *REFEREE calls a foul on FRANK.*

REFEREE   Round Six: "Members Only."

REFEREE begins the round. Slowly the men approach one another at centre. They face one another and make the sound of a telephone. They return to their briefcases, open them, pull out cell phones.

FRANK & BILL   Yeah? Oh hello Sir! Yes Sir.

FRANK   Thank you Sir.

BILL   I'm sorry Sir.

FRANK   Thank you Sir.

BILL   I'm sorry Sir.

FRANK   Thank you Sir.

BILL   I'm sorry Sir.

FRANK   Ha ha ha!

BILL   I... I... I...

FRANK   Thank you—

BILL   I'm sorry—

FRANK   Bobby.

BILL   Sir.

FRANK and BILL hang up. Slowly they approach one another at centre. They face one another and make the sound of a telephone. They return to their phones once again.

FRANK & BILL   Yeah?
Hi. I'm in the middle of something right now. Can I.... Can I.... Can I call you back?
I don't know.
I told you that. Yes I did. Yes I did this morning. Well it's not my fault if you don't listen. That's right. When I get there.

They hang up.

BILL   Sally says "Hi."

FRANK   Donna says "Hi."

FRANK & BILL   Hi.

FRANK and BILL slowly approach centre. They meet and turn to face the REFEREE, their backs to the audience. They take out their penises for inspection. After some deliberation she calls a tie. Relieved BILL and FRANK tuck in their gear, turn and step forward.

No one is perfect.

BILL   By William (Bill) Wade

FRANK   and A. Francis DeLorenzo. No one is perfect.

BILL   No one. Were our fathers perfect? Certainly not.

FRANK   Were our mothers perfect?

FRANK & BILL   Perhaps.

BILL   But I am not my mother.

FRANK & BILL   No.

FRANK   Nor is my wife my mother.

BILL   No.

FRANK   Nor will she ever be as much as I might wish she were as hard as she might try.

BILL   Frank?

FRANK   I digress.
Am I perfect?

BILL   Am I perfect?

FRANK & BILL   No.

FRANK   Yet, let us consider a moment—

BILL   —a moment—

FRANK   —that I am not myself—

BILL   —myself—

FRANK   —but rather—

FRANK & BILL   —someone else.

FRANK   Then as this person—

BILL   —I could—

FRANK   —watch me—

BILL   —take note—

FRANK   —take note—

FRANK & BILL   —of all the things I do—

BILL   —the small selfishness—

FRANK   —the minor idiosyncrasies—

FRANK & BILL   —the tiny spaces—

BILL   —between me—

FRANK & BILL   —and perfection.

FRANK   Perhaps then it would—

FRANK & BILL   —be e... be e... be easier—

BILL   —to see—

FRANK   —to look at me—

BILL   —and see—

FRANK & BILL   —be e... be e... be easier—

FRANK   —to change.

FRANK & BILL   But of course if I was someone else I would have my own problems to deal with.

FRANK   So what is perfect?

BILL   What?

FRANK   Besides tomorrow.

FRANK & BILL   Ah tomorrow!

BILL   Because tomorrow is an endless possibility—

FRANK & BILL   —and an endless possibility is the second best thing to wake up next to.

FRANK   But what? Let us consider a moment...

BILL   ...a note.

FRANK & BILL   A note.

BILL Laaaaaaaaaaaaaaaa aaaaaaaaaaaaaaaaaaaaaaaaaaaa aaaaaaaaaaaaaaaaaaaaaaaaaaaa aaaaaaaaaaaaaaaaaaaaaaaaaaaa aaaaaaaaaaaaaaaaaaaaaaaaaaaa aaa.	**FRANK** At first faltering and self-conscious then building up then pushed forward then gaining commitment then losing breath and trailing off near the end.

BILL   But in it there was something—

FRANK & BILL   —perfect.

FRANK   A happy accident?

BILL   A fluke?

FRANK   Mere chance?

FRANK & BILL   Perhaps. But back to me.

FRANK   And me—

BILL   —for all my weakness—

FRANK   —as a note—

FRANK & BILL   —let's say—

BILL   —a note stretched out from birth—

FRANK & BILL   —to death,

FRANK   I will allow—

BILL   —that here and there—

FRANK   —from time to time—

BILL   —there is a sound—

FRANK   —a thought—

BILL   —a word—

FRANK & BILL   —that touches on perfection.

BILL   But overall—

FRANK   —and wholly, no—

FRANK & BILL   —I know—

FRANK   —I am not perfect.

FRANK & BILL   I know—

BILL   —I am not perfect.

FRANK & BILL   But as not perfect as I am he's a whole hell of a lot more not perfect than me.

> *FRANK and BILL resume their seats.*

REFEREE   Half-time.

> *REFEREE comes down centre.*

This is the beach. Here is the bay. There is the point.

> *FRANK and BILL come down and join her on either side.*

REFEREE   This is the beach.
Here is the bay.
There is the point.
This is the beach.
Here is the bay.
There is the point.
This is the beach.

FRANK & BILL   On the beach.
At the bay.
On the beach.
At the bay.
On the beach.
At the bay.

REFEREE	FRANK & BILL
Here is the bay.	On the beach at the bay.
There is the point.	On the beach at the bay.
Race you to the point?	On the beach at the bay.
Sun.	
Boys.	
Sand.	
Water.	
Summer.	

FRANK   On the beach at the bay.

BILL   Every day that summer.

FRANK   On the beach at the bay.

BILL   All day every day.

FRANK   On the beach at the bay.

BILL   Every day that summer.

FRANK   On the beach at the bay.

BILL   All summer long.

REFEREE   It is the last day of summer before school begins. Two boys and the girl. She lies in the sun in her blue bathing suit on her green beach towel with her yellow radio. And I could tell you little things about her. I could tell you that her name was Lisa. I could tell you that she had a big brother. I could tell you that she loved horses and lilacs and going to the movies. But that doesn't matter now, all that matters is she is here on the beach with the two boys. The boys watch the girl. She stares out past the point to where the sea makes a line on the sky. The boys are silent and shy. She can hear them blush. She reminds one boy of his sister, she reminds the other of a picture of a woman he once saw in a magazine. The boys simply watch the girl.

> *FRANK and BILL sing a verse of a summer song.*

The sun hangs about there, just over the point. She is a little drowsy. She gets up and wanders to the edge of the water. She looks out. She feels a breeze. She turns her head a little over her shoulder and speaks to the boys:
"Race you to the point?"

> *Through the following the girl walks to the edge of the stage, they slowly assume racing positions.*

This is the beach.
Here is the bay.

There is the point.
This is the beach.
Here is the bay.
There is the point.
There is...

FRANK & BILL   On the beach.
At the bay.

REFEREE   There is...

FRANK & BILL   On the beach at the bay.

REFEREE   There is...

FRANK & BILL   On the beach at the bay.

REFEREE   There is...

FRANK & BILL   On the beach at the bay.

REFEREE   There is the point.

FRANK   And we sat—

BILL   —on the sand—

FRANK   —at the edge—

BILL   —of the point—

FRANK   —and we waited—

BILL   —and waited...

REFEREE   Race you to the point? Do you remember?

FRANK   One.

BILL   Two.

REFEREE   I remember too.
I remember. Three!

> *REFEREE resumes her position on chair. She blows her whistle to end half-time. The MEN return to their chairs.*

Recap: Two men enter a room. A taller man and a shorter man. And each man carries a briefcase. The first man seems very much like the second man and the second man seems very much like the first man but they are not.

FRANK & BILL   No.

REFEREE   They are not for two reasons. One: one man is the first man and two: one man in his briefcase has a gun.

BILL   A gun.

FRANK   A gun.

REFEREE   Which man is the first man and which man has the gun?
Round Seven: "Dad."

> *REFEREE begins the round. FRANK and BILL approach one another*
> *at centre. FRANK does the "what's-on-your-tie" gag to BILL, ending*
> *in a nose flick. BILL shoves FRANK. FRANK shoves BILL. BILL*
> *shoves FRANK knocking him down. REFEREE calls a foul on BILL.*
> *FRANK and BILL circle one another.*

FRANK   How's your dad?

BILL   Why?

FRANK   I always liked your dad.

BILL   Really?

FRANK   Yeah.

BILL   Well. I always liked your dad.

FRANK   Really?

BILL   Yeah.

FRANK & BILL   Gee.

FRANK   Your dad was a real easy going guy.

BILL   Your dad was a real card.

FRANK   Your dad was a real dreamer.

BILL   Your dad was a real character.

FRANK   Your dad was a real nice guy.

BILL   He was a real maniac.

FRANK   He was a real boozer.

BILL   Ha. He was a real wild man.

FRANK   A real cuckold.

BILL   A real wiener.

FRANK   A real dick.

BILL   A real prick.

FRANK   A lemming.

BILL   A fascist.

FRANK   An ass.

BILL   A pig!
How's your mom?

> *REFEREE ends the round. She calls a tie.*
> *FRANK and BILL speak simultaneously, the capitalized phrases time*
> *out to be spoken in unison.*

FRANK   Please be warned that if
you think I'm going to stand
here and start dishing dirt and
airing laundry about
HIS FATHER.
I won't.
But let's just say the despera-
tion he displays comes from
HIS FATHER.
Not that I'm sure he wasn't
a well-intentioned ill-educated
man but, and education isn't
everything but
FOR EXAMPLE:
Rather than face the
criminal charges
HIS FATHER
implied
he could not multiply
eight times nine when
HIS FATHER
's company was missing some
seventy-two thousand dollars
at the year-end audit.
HIS FATHER
claimed he had marked down
twenty four. Twenty four? Give
me a break.
AND THAT'S JUST ONE
EXAMPLE.
Dishonest?
Well he did admit to an
ignorance in arithmetic and—
WELL I'M SURE YOU KNOW
WHAT THEY SAY ABOUT
FATHERS AND SONS

BILL   Now this is more than
name calling here although of
course that is the temptation
but
HIS FATHER
drove his mother crazy.
I mean she did have a drinking
problem but
HIS FATHER
didn't help at all. She spent
the last fifteen years in and
out of detox as a result of his
antics.
FOR EXAMPLE:
At the Girl Guide Boy Scout
banquet in grade eight
HIS FATHER
was supposed to make
a presentation but when the
time came
HIS FATHER
was nowhere to be found.
Twenty minutes later five guys
from the sixth pack found
HIS FATHER
in the boiler room with Suzie
Walsh a sixteen-year-old
Girl Guide.
AND THAT'S JUST ONE
EXAMPLE.
Is he like that?
Well they say a guy and his
father are—
WELL I'M SURE YOU KNOW
WHAT THEY SAY ABOUT
FATHERS AND SONS

FRANK —and far be it, far be it indeed for me to say that HE IS THE PERFECT EXAMPLE. THANK YOU.	**BILL** —and I'm not saying they're right all the time, but in this case HE IS THE PERFECT EXAMPLE. THANK YOU.

REFEREE   Pardon me?

FRANK and BILL repeat the above at twice the speed.

Thank you.

FRANK & BILL   You're welcome.

REFEREE   Round Eight: "All In The Palm Of His Hand."

REFEREE begins the round. FRANK and BILL come to centre. FRANK takes out a cigar and lights it…. They face one another.

FRANK   You've got auction preferreds yielding seventy percent of prime and 50/51 up either side what do you want to do? Convert with three-year hard call protection, two-year pay back, the hedge is a lay up? I don't think so. I say capitalize the loss by rolling it into goodwill and amortizing over forty years. Of course profits will be decreased by the switch from FIFO to LIFO. And then remember Bethlehem! Where application of FASBY 87 meant balance sheet quality went way down because of the unfunded pension liability. I mean if we were in the clear I could offer at one half and give up an eighth to the market maker for three eighths net fill, but unfortunately we're not. Are you with me?

BILL takes FRANK's cigar and puts it out in the palm of his hand (this is a trick done by BILL palming silly putty which takes the heat of the burning cigar). REFEREE ends the round. She gives the victory to BILL. FRANK resumes his seat. BILL steps forward. As he speaks he stands in one position but points and steps and turns in place as indicated.

BILL   Let's go to my place everybody. Okay. Ready?
This is the back door.
We always use the back door.
Here is the rec room. There is the bar. There is the laundry room.
Hallway, stairs.
Going up stairs, going up stairs.
Out that window that's the yard.
Here's a hallway. There's the kitchen.
Microwave butcher's block breakfast nook.
Hallway.

Turn.
Dining room.
Oak table, eight chairs, hallway, French doors, living room.
It's sunken!
Big window.
Big skylight.
Grand
piano
(white).
Through the hallway into the foyer.
Front—
We never use the front door.
Window window Powder Room.
MASSIVE STAIRCASE!
One. Two. Three. Four. Five bedrooms. (Can in two).
Long hallway. Smaller staircase.
Going up stairs. Going up stairs. Going up stairs.
Door. Locked. Key. Open the door. And this
is my
secret room.

FRANK   I heard you rent.

> *REFEREE calls a foul on FRANK. BILL approaches FRANK.*

BILL   Where'd you hear that?

FRANK   Around.

BILL   Yeah?

FRANK   Yeah.

BILL   Around where?

FRANK   Just around.

BILL   Phil?

FRANK   Might've been Phil.

BILL   Phil's full of shit.

> *BILL returns to centre. This time as he speaks he stands and delivers the speech without moving.*

As I was saying.
This is my place.
Back door rec room bar laundry out that window that's the yard
kitchen hallway turn dining room turn living room turn hallway.
MASSIVE STAIRCASE

one two three four five bedrooms hallway staircase.
Going up stairs going up stairs going up stairs.
Door locked key open the door
and this is my secret room.
And this is my secret room.
And this is my secret room.
And it's empty except for a great big window right here, and when
I look out of it I see the tops of trees, and hills, black roads with white
lines, and a whole lake, and two kinds of earth: dark wet earth and clay,
and big green fields and sky that's only ever blue.
And all of it.
Everything.
Theskythefieldsthetreesthelakethehillstheroadtheclay.
Everything I see, and farther where you can't see, all of it, everything, is
mine.
It's all mine.

> *BILL resumes his seat.*

REFEREE   Round Nine: "Power Lunch."

> *FRANK and BILL bring their chairs centre. They sit facing one
> another with their briefcases on their laps. REFEREE begins the
> round.*

FRANK   Been here before?

BILL   Oh yeah.

FRANK   How's the steak?

BILL   Very good.

FRANK   How's the swordfish?

BILL   Very good

FRANK   How's the shark?

BILL   Greasy.

FRANK & BILL   Excuse me a second.

> *FRANK and BILL reach into their briefcases and take out their
> phones. They dial and both make a ringing sound. As BILL speaks
> FRANK continues to ring.*

BILL   Hi doll!
Listen sorry I was short with you before.
Did you go ahead and have dinner anyway?
Ahhh…. Well how bout I pick up a pizza on my way home?
And a movie?

Something funny?
Something romantic! That sounds nice!
Okay "Turnip."
I do you too.
Bye bye.

FRANK and BILL hang up.

How's Donna?

Pause.

How's—

FRANK   I heard you. She's very good.

BILL   Really?

FRANK   Yes. How's the spaghettini?

BILL   Oily. I saw Donna at the Fuller's party.

FRANK   Oh yes.

BILL   You weren't there.

FRANK   No I wasn't.

BILL   Phil was there.

FRANK   Was he?

BILL   He was having a good time.

FRANK   Good.

BILL   So was Donna.

FRANK   Donna likes a good—

BILL   Party?

FRANK   Yes.

BILL   I've heard that.

FRANK   How's the squid?

BILL   Sneaky.

FRANK   Sneaky?

BILL   Sneaks up on you. Nice tie.

FRANK   Yes you mentioned—

BILL   Somebody has good taste.

FRANK   How's Sally?

BILL   Very good.

FRANK   Really?

BILL   She was at the Fuller's.
Strange you weren't there.

FRANK   Well I wasn't.

BILL   Working late?

FRANK   I don't believe you've ever had the steak or the swordfish or the shark or the spaghettini or the squid here.

BILL   No I haven't. But it was some party.

REFEREE ends the round. She gives the victory to FRANK.

Bullshit call!

REFEREE calls a foul on BILL. BILL resumes his seat. FRANK steps forward.

FRANK   Let's not use the word "class." Class being such a nebulous word. Let's instead use the mountain. Mountain. And many men are born without a mountain. It is not a birthright. This is not to say that a mountain is particularly better than a valley—just as we may find from time to time that knowledge is not particularly better than ignorance. And even being second has its benefits. For example… less income tax? But some men live on mountains and some men live in valleys and if only those men standing small and insignificant in the valley would stop their futile fight to stake a claim at the crest of a hill they can never hope to own. If only they would not be so blind and for a moment consider the privilege of living in the benevolent shadow of a mountain. But to be brave enough to see that truth and face it, that takes balls, and like mountains many men are born without them.

BILL   Fuck you Alphonse.

REFEREE calls a foul on BILL.

FRANK   You slimy little—

REFEREE calls a foul on FRANK.

REFEREE   Round ten: "Business Ties."

*REFEREE begins the round. FRANK and BILL step centre.
FRANK faces the audience. BILL faces FRANK and stands at an uncomfortably close distance.*

FRANK   Now I don't want to harp on business Bill but I happen to be pretty tight with Bobby and Bobby runs everything and I know how things are with you and there's a chance that there might be a place opening up in accounting and from what I've heard—

BILL   Frank I really like that tie.

FRANK   And from what I've heard about business Bill—

BILL   Silk?
Of course.
How could I imagine Donna would buy a tie like that?

FRANK   I'm offering you a break here Bill I'm—

BILL   That's not Donna's taste.
Very flashy.
Yet tasteful.
Where would a person buy a tie like that?
What kind of store?

FRANK   Bill…

BILL   What kind of person would go into that kind of store and buy a tie like that?

FRANK   Don't Bill.

BILL   A very young tie!

FRANK   Shut up about the goddamn tie!

> *FRANK resumes his seat. REFEREE ends the round. She gives the victory to BILL. BILL steps forward.*

BILL   Two stories. The first story is a very familiar story because everybody knows it. And it's a story about a little temp, eighteen years old, who is, by the way, knocked up and who happens to have not bad taste in ties don't you think? And the second story is a secret so just keep it to yourselves. We're at the Fuller's party. Me and Sally. Huge spread, packed bar, beautiful house, the works. Tons of people, people everywhere. There's Donna! Where's Frank? Frank's not here. Donna's there though. She looks great! Who's that she's talking to? It's Phil. I wander over. They're talking about politics. I wander off. Have a drink, have a chat, check out the pool, come back in, poke around some more at the buffet, shoot the shit… Phil and Donna still talking! I cruise over. Now they're talking about poetry. I cruise off. Time comes to go Sally's pulling on my arm I'm talking to Mister Fuller. Look around for Donna to say goodbye…. No Donna. Look around for Phil…. No Phil. I gotta take a pee before we leave, walk in the can. There's Donna. In the shower. With Phil. And when she sees me she smiles and says: "Shh! Come on in and close the door Bill." Now the first story you can repeat but the second story, that's a secret.

BILL resumes his seat.

REFEREE   Round Eleven: "My Boy."

REFEREE begins the round. FRANK and BILL step to centre. They do a simple choreography of hand gestures.

FRANK & BILL   Let me tell you something about my boy...

FRANK, flummoxed, does the wrong gesture.

FRANK   Sorry.

FRANK & BILL   Let me tell you something about my boy.
He's a good boy, my boy.
A good boy, a smart boy.
He's the best boy my boy.
No question, he's the best—

FRANK makes another error.

BILL   *(to FRANK)* Are you with us?

FRANK & BILL   Let me tell you something about my boy...

FRANK again makes an error. FRANK steps away. REFEREE moves to end the round. BILL stops her.

BILL   What's your problem? Hey. Hey. What's your problem?

BILL looks at the audience, shrugging.

FRANK   Password.

BILL does not respond.

Password!

BILL does not respond.

Winner rules.

BILL   That's not in the game.

FRANK steps to centre.

FRANK   Password.

BILL joins him at centre.

BILL   Winner rules.

FRANK and BILL do a childhood handshake.

FRANK & BILL Cut!
Spit!
Mix! Brothers brothers never part,
no broken vows or covered hearts,
in all our weakness, all our woes
we stick together, highs and lows.

FRANK Pledge?

BILL Made.

FRANK Promise?

BILL Kept.

FRANK To what end?

BILL Never end. Transit! Transport!

> *FRANK and BILL join hands, arms raised over their heads, forming an arch. The REFEREE walks through this and down centre.*

One.

FRANK Two.

REFEREE Three.

> *FRANK, BILL and the REFEREE begin a "swimming" action.*

FRANK, BILL & REFEREE
Cut through the water to the point. Cut through the water to the point. Cut through the water to the point. Cut through the water to the point.

> *The three continue the "action," and the MEN continue the above as:*

REFEREE I'll beat you.
I'm a good swimmer.
You guys think you're so hot.
My brother taught me to swim and he's on a team.
What's your names anyway?
My name's Lisa.
My mom calls me Leelee but I hate that.
What's your names anyway?
You guys got a cottage here?
You brothers?
We've got a cottage up by the store on the hill, you know where
I mean? It used to be a farm but we don't have any animals. I wish
we had a horse, I love horses. I go to the movie on Sunday. I go every
Sunday even if it's one I saw already. Hey slow down it's far. Slow
down.

REFEREE   What's your names?

FRANK & BILL

FRANK & BILL
And I feel her fall back.
And I feel her fall back.

REFEREE   What's your names?
Hey.
Wait.
Let's not race.
Wait.
We're too far.
Slow down.
Hey.
Wait.
Hey…

FRANK & BILL
And I feel her fall back.
And I feel her fall back.
And I feel her fall back.
And I feel her fall back.
And I feel her fall back.
And I feel her fall back.
And I feel her fall back.
And I feel her fall back.

FRANK and BILL continue the above while:

REFEREE   His decision.
His compassion.
His desire.
His jealousy.
His guilt.
His self-image.
His self-knowledge.
His self-loathing.
His fear of death.
His weakness.
His pride.
His power.

FRANK continues the swimming action forward while BILL stops and turns.

FRANK   Cut through the water
to the point.
Cut through the water
to the point.
Cut through the water
to the point.
Cut through the water
to the point.

BILL   And I feel her I feel her
fall back.
And I feel her I feel her
fall back.
And I feel her I feel her
fall back.
And I feel her I feel her
fall back.

The men are silent as:

REFEREE   And first there is panic.
And so much sound.
Rushing.
Swirling.
Pulsing.
And then no sound. And then peace. And then you will float or you

will sink. And if you float you will be as if flying and if you sink, when you hit bottom, you will bounce like a man on the moon.

BILL turns and rejoins FRANK in the swimming action.

FRANK & BILL   Cut through the water to the point.
Cut through the water to the point.
Cut through the water to the point.
Cut through the water to the point.

> *FRANK slowly rises his arms in victory. BILL continues to "swim." The REFEREE returns to her chair. FRANK walks toward BILL. BILL continues to "swim."*

BILL   Cut through the water to the point. Cut through the water to the point. Cut through the water to the point. Cut through the water to the point.

> *BILL rises as he continues to speak. FRANK places his hand on BILL's shoulder.*

Cut through the water to the point. Cut through the water to the point. Cut through the water to the point. Cut through the water to the point.

> *FRANK and BILL are now standing face to face. With his other hand FRANK punches BILL in the stomach. BILL goes down. REFEREE ends the round. She gives the victory to FRANK. BILL struggles to his feet and approaches FRANK. FRANK addresses the audience.*

FRANK   I'd like to make a few things clear. These are my ears, these are my eyes, this is the back of my hand.

> *FRANK strikes BILL with the back of his hand. BILL goes down.*

And the winner has, and will always, rule.
That is the way of the world. Like battle, like business, like love. A few may fall along the way but compared to the prize what are a few. And the prize is what you want and what you want is what you hear in every mouth, every buzz, every bell, every crack, every whisper: "me, my, mine." Don't be afraid. The thing we must learn is how to balance compassion and desire. For example: Bill? You like this tie?

> *FRANK takes his tie off and puts it around BILL's neck.*

Have it.

> *FRANK yanks on the tie.*

Say thank you.
Say thank you!

BILL   (*choking*) Thank you.

FRANK drops BILL to the floor.

FRANK   No thanks necessary Bill, I've got a dozen just like it at home. You see. Don't be fooled.

FRANK lifts BILL and supports him.

Beware compassion. Compassion will lose the race. Compassion is illogical. If you let it compassion will kill desire. Especially the desire to be first. And being first my friends is the point.

FRANK throws BILL across the stage.

Compassion is the brother of guilt.

FRANK lifts BILL by his tie.

And guilt is the mother of stomach cancer.

FRANK knees BILL in the stomach.

The first man is the man...

FRANK knees BILL in the chest. BILL goes down.

...who is guiltless beyond all circumstance...

FRANK kicks BILL.

...and sure of his right...

FRANK kicks BILL.

...to be first.

FRANK kicks BILL.

The first man is the man...

FRANK kicks BILL.

...who can recognize the second man.

BILL lies motionless. FRANK steps forward.

And we sat on the sand at the edge of the point and we waited and we waited and you got scared and you ran home and all night long I waited and in the morning when her body washed up on the shore I tried to comfort her but she did not respond, then to evoke some reaction I slapped her so hard my hand still hurts. And then learning my lesson I declared myself first to the point.

FRANK resumes his seat.

REFEREE   Round Twelve: "Rumours of Glory."

FRANK steps to centre. BILL tries to struggle to his feet. REFEREE calls a foul on BILL. BILL continues to struggle. REFEREE calls

> *a foul on BILL. BILL continues to struggle. REFEREE ends the round. She gives the victory to FRANK. FRANK steps forward. BILL manages to get to his feet. He approaches his briefcase.*

FRANK   I have always been, will always be, the first.

> *FRANK resumes his seat. BILL opens his briefcase, takes out a gun, aims it at FRANK.*

BILL   And I learned my lesson Frank, I won't be second again.

> *FRANK, surprised, opens his briefcase. Frank takes out a gun and aims it at BILL.*

(to REFEREE) There was only supposed to be one gun!

REFEREE   *(to BILL)* I guess somebody lied.

> *The REFEREE steps forward and addresses the audience.*

The two men will stand here just like this for a long time to come with one thought. One thought racing through each man's mind:

FRANK & BILL   Somebody lied.
Somebody lied.
Somebody lied.

> *The REFEREE steps down and to centre carrying a yellow transistor. The men continue to speak "somebody lied" through the following.*

REFEREE   Two boys on a beach. The last day of summer before school begins. Nearby is a girl. She lies in the sun in her blue bathing suit on her green beach towel listening to her yellow radio. She reminds one boy of his sister, she reminds the other of a picture of a woman he once saw in a magazine. The sun hangs about there. Just over the point. She turns her head a little over her shoulder and speaks to the boys: "Race you to the point?"

> *The MEN stop speaking.*

And they do.
One two three.
The boys are afraid.
The boys are still afraid.
Round Thirteen:

> *The MEN cock their guns.*

Only one gun is loaded.

> *She whistles to begin the round. The men look at her in disbelief still keeping aim. She places the radio on the stage, turns it on. She exits the way the men came in. The radio plays a happy beach song. The*

men look at one another still keeping aim.
Lights fade.
The End.

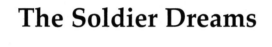

The Soldier Dreams

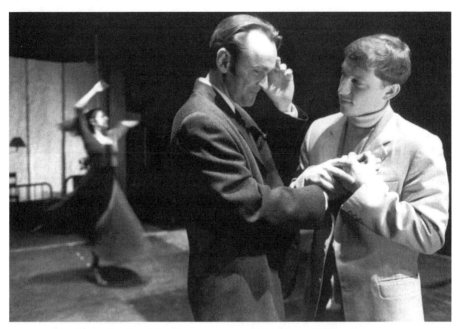

l to r: Heather MacCrimmon, Daniel MacIvor, Volker Burger
photo by Jacques Oulé

The Soldier Dreams was originally produced by da da kamera and premiered at Canadian Stage Company, Toronto, in March 1997 with the following company:

DAVID (1) . . . . John McLachlin
DAVID . . . . Daniel MacIvor
TISH . . . . Caroline Gillis
SAM . . . . Jim Allodi
JUDY . . . . Heather MacCrimmon
RICHARD . . . . Blair Williams
STUDENT . . . . Volker Bürger
NURSE . . . . Carol Gillis

Directed by Daniel Brooks and Daniel MacIvor
Dramaturged by Daniel Brooks
Set and Light Design by Jan Komárek
Sound and Music Composed by Richard Feren
Produced by Sherrie Johnson
Assisted by Rochelle Hum

Characters

DAVID (1) is the dying David. He is surrounded by his care team: his lover RICHARD, his younger sister JUDY, his older sister TISH, her husband SAM. DAVID is the memory David—he exists in the past with the German medical STUDENT.

Note well: in the text of the play the dying David will be denoted by "DAVID (1)"—the memory David will be simply "DAVID."

Setting

In our Toronto productions DAVID (1) in his bed dominated the space; we used no other furniture at all, but I think there are many choices between realism and minimalism for the bedroom scenes.

On either side of the bed and outside the area that we defined as DAVID's "room" were two raised platforms and on each was a microphone on a stand. On these platforms the memory scenes took place. It felt right that DAVID and the STUDENT should be an unrealistic distance apart—the microphones also helped to remove the action from the bedside scenes—more memory-like or dream-like. It wasn't until the final memory "Ottawa. Apartment. Morning." that DAVID and the STUDENT played out the scene with a physical realism.

The Soldier Dreams

A requiem plays as the audience enters.
DAVID (1) lies motionless in the bed. The light fades and the Soldier's
theme plays. The STUDENT passes through the space. He pauses and
looks at DAVID (1). He exits the space. Slowly DAVID's family
enters the room one by one. First TISH followed by SAM then JUDY
and finally RICHARD. The four stand around the bed. DAVID enters
the space and addresses the audience.

DAVID   Hello I'm David. These are some people I know. My big sister
Tish, her husband Sam, my little sister Judy, my lover Richard. And the
guy in the bed, that's me. And if I had my way we'd all be dancing.

> *The music swells and DAVID exits. The NURSE enters, sits on the*
> *edge of the bed and begins working on DAVID (1). DAVID (1)*
> *groans.*

SAM   Should we be here?

RICHARD   No we should be anywhere but here.

SAM   Right...

> *DAVID (1) groans.*

TISH   *(to JUDY)* What is she doing?

NURSE   I'm inserting the drip line into the catheter in his chest.

> *DAVID (1) groans.*

TISH   Why is he making that noise?

SAM   Is he in pain or?...

TISH   Watch his arm. That's his sore arm.

SAM   Does he need a painkiller?

TISH   Is he due for another painkiller?

RICHARD   No but I am.

TISH   *(to RICHARD)* What's that supposed to mean? *(to NURSE)* Watch
his arm.

JUDY   Guys. Let's let the nurse do her job.

> *Silence.*

DAVID (1)   Ottawa.

NURSE   Ottawa?

RICHARD   Ottawa right Ottawa.

SAM   Ottawa.

JUDY   *(to NURSE)* He's saying that a lot.

TISH   He's remembering our wedding.

RICHARD   Your wedding?

SAM   Did something special happen at our wedding?

TISH   Yeah, we got married.

SAM   *(to TISH)* Sorry.

RICHARD   He's probably just delirious.

TISH   He was Sam's best man.

SAM   Yeah.

TISH   He looked so nice.

DAVID (1)   Matchbook.

SAM   Matchbook yeah matchbook. He says that a lot too. *(to NURSE)* What do you suppose it means?

TISH   How would she know?

SAM   No I know just…

NURSE   Does he smoke?

RICHARD   No.   **TISH**   Yes.

RICHARD   *(to TISH)* He quit.

NURSE   That might have something to do with it. *(to JUDY)* These pyjamas?

TISH   Yes?

NURSE   I think they might be giving him a rash.

TISH   What? No, that's impossible, they're a hundred percent cotton.

NURSE   Yes but—see how it's red here? Cotton can be a little rough.

JUDY   We'll change them. Thanks.

    The NURSE exits.

SAM   He's got a bit more colour today though. Than yesterday.

TISH   *(to JUDY re: NURSE)* You checked her references?

JUDY   Yes. She's good.

TISH   Did you see the way she moved his sore arm?

SAM   Which one?   **JUDY**   Which arm?

TISH   I think we should look for someone else.

JUDY   I like her.

TISH   Judy, discernment has never been your strong point.

JUDY   *(moves to the door)* I'm going to get David a change of pyjamas.

TISH   *(to JUDY)* Are we going to deal with this nurse thing?

JUDY   I like the nurse.

TISH   You like her, fine take her to a movie.

JUDY   You don't have to like her she's not your nurse.

TISH   And she's not yours either.

RICHARD   Why don't we ask David what he thinks. *(loudly)* David honey? Do you like your nurse?

JUDY   Richard!

TISH   Shhh!

RICHARD   *(to DAVID (1))* Do you think she's competent? *(to TISH)* Well it looks like he's not going to rise out of his coma to tell us.

> *RICHARD exits. TISH gives JUDY a look. JUDY exits. TISH gives SAM a look. SAM shrugs his shoulders. TISH exits. SAM is alone with DAVID. SAM approaches the bed and looks down upon the silent DAVID (1).*

DAVID   Ottawa.

> *Light cross fades from the bed to DAVID and the STUDENT.*

The Airport. A cab. Night.

STUDENT   Hello.

DAVID   Hello. You're going downtown?

> *The STUDENT nods.*

I guess we'll just split the fare or whatever.

> *The STUDENT gives him a strange look.*

Oh, it looks like the rain is stopping.

STUDENT   *(offering)* Cigarette?

DAVID   I don't think you're allowed to... um.... Sure.

> *DAVID takes a cigarette from the STUDENT. (In the original production DAVID palmed the cigarette and when the STUDENT*

offered it, it magically appeared in his hand.) The STUDENT lights a match from a matchbook and offers to light DAVID's cigarette.

No thanks I quit. I just like to hold it.

The STUDENT gives him a strange look. Pause.

Are you from Hamburg?

STUDENT   Pardon?

DAVID   Your matchbook says...

STUDENT   Oh yes, no I'm from Berlin.

DAVID   Oh.

STUDENT   I visit Hamburg from time to time.

DAVID   Where do you live in Berlin?

STUDENT   Do you know Berlin?

DAVID   No but I.... Right.

STUDENT   I live here now. For one year. I am a student.

DAVID   Oh studying?...

STUDENT   Yes.

DAVID   No I mean what do you want to be?

STUDENT   "Want to be?"

DAVID   Um.... What job are you studying to obtain?

STUDENT   A doctor.

DAVID   Ahh. *(laughs at his inadvertent joke)* "Ahh." *(He does it again, sticking out his tongue and putting his head back, so that he will "get it.")* "Ahhhh."

> *The STUDENT gives him a strange look, smiles weakly, turns away After a moment he gets it.*

STUDENT   *(laughing)* Ah! *(sticking out his tongue)* "Ahhh."

> *They laugh together. A pause.*

It's a nice night.

DAVID   Yes it is.

STUDENT   Perhaps we could walk.

> *Pause.*

DAVID   From the airport?

STUDENT   I mean have a walk. Take a walk. Show me your Ottawa?

DAVID   Ah.

STUDENT   "Ahhh."

DAVID   "Ahhh."

DAVID & STUDENT   "Ahhh."

> *They laugh together.*
> *Light crossfades to the bedroom. SAM and JUDY in the bedroom.*
> *SAM makes notes in a little book. JUDY holds an unlit cigarette.*

TISH   Did you talk to that girl?

JUDY   What girl?

TISH   The nurse.

JUDY   No.

TISH   Are you going to talk to her?

JUDY   No.

TISH   Well someone's going to have to talk to her.

JUDY   I don't have a problem with her.

TISH   Someone's going to have to talk to her.

JUDY   Don't look at me.

> *TISH looks at SAM.*

SAM   Maybe you should talk to her.

TISH   What's the point. She wouldn't listen to me. She clearly doesn't like me.

JUDY   I wonder why.

TISH   She's antagonistic.

SAM   I think she's nice.

TISH   You think everyone's nice.

JUDY   Maybe everyone is.

TISH   Right.

JUDY   Maybe everyone's just scared.

> *Pause.*

TISH   *(to JUDY)* When did you start smoking?

JUDY   After Mom died.

TISH   That's smart.

JUDY   Somebody's got to carry the torch.

TISH   You're not going to smoke it in here.

JUDY   Hardly.

>   *Pause.*

TISH   Do you want some JELL-O?

>   *JUDY groans.*

(to SAM) Do you want some JELL-O?

SAM   No thanks.

>   *RICHARD enters laughing. He carries a card and two lottery tickets.*

RICHARD   What are these?

TISH   Sorry?

RICHARD   These.

TISH   Lottery tickets?

RICHARD   Lottery tickets! From your cousins! People send cards, people send flowers, people send notes or chocolates or fruit or prayers even. People do not send lottery tickets. However, your cousins do. And not to mention all the other idiots I've been... I have been on the phone all afternoon, everybody wants a piece of it: people he used to work with, his old boss, his hairdresser, his accountant, old boyfriends—where do these people come from, the person from the corner store called! The person we sold that carpet to, the people we rented that cottage from... it's ridiculous.

>   *TISH stares icily at RICHARD.*

What?

TISH   People care, is that a problem?

RICHARD   People are vultures.

TISH   That's a nice attitude.

>   *TISH exits.*

RICHARD   She really doesn't get it.

SAM   No she gets it, she's just Tish.

RICHARD   Well she doesn't get me.

SAM   No no she thinks you're great.

JUDY snorts.
RICHARD gives SAM a look.

Well no not "great" but she doesn't, you know despise you or anything.

RICHARD   That's good to know.

RICHARD exits.

JUDY   "She thinks you're great?"

SAM shrugs.
Blackout on JUDY and SAM.
A spotlight up on TISH who addresses the audience.

TISH   Hello I'm Tish, David's big sister. Tish, that's short for Trish, which is short for Patricia. It was Trish until David started to talk, but he couldn't say Trish he could only say Tish and so it stuck and so it's Tish. And so… I would like to take this moment for David. Of course if David had his way we'd probably all be dancing. David has always been quite the dancing fool—not me though—I could barely work up a shimmy at my own wedding reception. I guess it's safe to say there is no "dancing gene." I mean, that's to say it doesn't run in the family. Although Judy's been known to shake her leg a bit. I guess when they were handing out rhythm I was… shopping. Ha ha. *(pause)* Anyway. Maybe if he gets a little better, we'll do a little samba 'round the bed. But what I wanted to say *(clears her throat)* Excuse me. What I wanted to do was tell a funny little story: When we were kids we weren't allowed to talk at the dinner table. Dad used to say "Digestion not discussion." And because we weren't allowed to talk at dinner it made it difficult not to—for David and me at least—not so much for Judy because she was just a baby and anyway whatever Dad said was the law for her she was always Daddy's little girl. *(pause)* Anyway! We weren't allowed to talk at the dinner table—and then it turned out that in Girl Guides I learned the sign alphabet—which was one of the few things I managed to learn from Girl Guides other than don't even think of putting me in a beret. Just call me Big Head. Ha ha. So. I taught David how to sign the alphabet and then at dinner we were able to communicate—you know, very surreptitiously, just small, like this. Not whole phrases or sentences or whatever of course, just… like a code which sort of deteriorated down into just mostly: W.F. Which stood for "Who Farted." And there were variations on that like Y.F. for "You Farted" and H.F. for "He Farted"—and there was also S.D.A. for "She's Drunk Again"—ha ha, poor old Mom. But um mostly W.F. So. Anyway…. But the thing is. The point is about the connection that David and I have. This secret little language we created back then represents—something special. Something private. Just for us.

Something special that I would never be able to have with anyone else. And also of course it talks about David and what a funny—what a wonderful sense of humour he had—he has—and you know, things like that. I hope that story wasn't, didn't seem coarse or.... Anyway. Thank you.

> *Spot fades on TISH.*
> *Light snaps up in the bedroom. JUDY, SAM and RICHARD are there.*

SAM   And the guy—the guy leans over the table and the doctor reaches in and he pulls out a dozen roses and the doctor says to the guy, "Do you know you have a dozen roses up your butt?" And the guy says, "Read the card! Read the card!"

> *RICHARD and JUDY do not respond.*

JUDY   Um.

SAM   *(to JUDY)* "Read the card!"

JUDY   The doctor said that?

SAM   No, the guy.

JUDY   Oh the roses were for the doctor!

SAM   From the guy!

JUDY   *(laughing)* Oh that's funny.

RICHARD   I don't think it's funny.

SAM   Well it's.... Why not?

RICHARD   I think it's bordering on homophobic actually.

SAM   No it's... no... I... Why?

RICHARD   It's a "gay" joke. The fact that it exists is offensive—like a "Polish" joke or a "Jew" joke. The content is irrelevant.

SAM   But, well, I didn't make it up.

RICHARD   Yes but you tell it.

SAM   But, well.... But the person who told me was gay.

RICHARD   Well that doesn't surprise me—homosexuals are notoriously homophobic.

SAM   Well? So? Sorry, you mean?...

RICHARD   I'm not accusing you. I'm just saying we have to watch out for these insidious little things.

SAM   Uh... right.

JUDY   The thing about the joke that sort of threw me was the "butt."

SAM   What?

JUDY   That the doctor said "Roses up your butt." Would a doctor say "butt"? Wouldn't a doctor say "rectum" or something.

SAM   Yeah but—rectum's not funny.

JUDY   I think rectum's funny, I think rectum's hilarious.

RICHARD   Irregardless of the wording it's still offensive.

JUDY   Oh Richard.

TISH enters.

TISH   Where is that carpet?

RICHARD   Which carpet?

TISH   Mom's carpet that David had in the storage closet upstairs.

JUDY   Oh yeah that carpet.

RICHARD   What were you doing in the storage closet?

TISH   Looking for the carpet. Where is it?

RICHARD   I'm not sure.

TISH   It's a very valuable carpet.

RICHARD   Well it's David's so…

TISH   Actually it's mine. David was keeping it for me. Mom gave it to me.

JUDY   When?

TISH   Ages ago. Before Dad died.

JUDY   Oh.

TISH   I'd just like to know where it is.

RICHARD   You'll have to—I don't know—maybe in the basement.

TISH   The basement? Doesn't your basement flood?

JUDY   Oh that's not good.

TISH   It's a very valuable carpet.

RICHARD   You said that already, what are you getting at.

Pause.

TISH   I'm not "getting at" anything—it's—I—We have room for it now and I thought we'd take it with us when we leave.

RICHARD   You're leaving?

TISH   No—I mean—Eventually we'll be leaving.

SAM   We don't need—we've got carpets and there's that floor painting thing you said you wanted to do in the den—

TISH   *(to RICHARD)* I'd just like to see it.

RICHARD   Well I'm sorry but it has nothing to do with me okay.

TISH   Look—

RICHARD   Don't "look" me.

JUDY   Guys...

> *The NURSE enters and sits on the bed.*

NURSE   Hello.

JUDY   Hi.

> *RICHARD exits. TISH gives JUDY a look re: talking to NURSE.*

Excuse me.

> *TISH gives SAM a look re: NURSE.*

SAM   Um. I'll just. Excuse me.

> *SAM exits. TISH turns away to prepare herself to speak to the NURSE.*

NURSE   *(to DAVID (1))* How are we doing?

TISH   *(turning to NURSE)* Well actually not too well since you ask... *(turns and realizes the NURSE is talking to DAVID)* Oh. I thought. I'm sorry...

> *The NURSE looks at TISH and then back to DAVID (1).*

NURSE   *(to DAVID (1), re: rash)* Oh that's looking a lot better. *(taking DAVID (1)'s hand)* It's a beautiful night out.

> *TISH watches the NURSE and DAVID (1).*
> *Light fades down to TISH and then crosses to the STUDENT and DAVID.*

STUDENT   Beautiful.

DAVID   Yes, I like this place.

STUDENT   Ottawa is new to me. You know Ottawa well?

DAVID   Not really. Just a few bars, and this spot.

STUDENT   There are many men in this park.

DAVID   Um. Well. Yeah…

    Pause.

My sister's getting married. Tomorrow. She lives here. In Ottawa. That's why I'm here.

STUDENT   That's wonderful.

DAVID   Well the guy she's marrying is a bit of a geek but—

STUDENT   A "Geek?"

DAVID   Um, yeah, um…

STUDENT   Weird?

DAVID   Yeah, weird.

STUDENT   Weird can be good.

DAVID   Yeah, weird can be good. I'm the best man.

STUDENT   Best of what?

DAVID   No for a wedding there's a… never mind.

STUDENT   Oh yes of course.

    Pause.

The water is so still.

DAVID   The lights are beautiful.

STUDENT   Yes. More so in the water. Of their reflection. This is the difference between a reality and a memory. The reflection is the memory of the light. The memory is always more wonderful.

DAVID   Not always.

STUDENT   Ah, now you speak from desire.

    Pause.

DAVID   I should go.

STUDENT   To a bar?

DAVID   A bar?

STUDENT   Okay.

DAVID   Oh… 'kay.

    Lights fade out on DAVID and the STUDENT then cross to the bedroom.
    SAM and RICHARD stand near the bed. Silence.

SAM   "We seek certainty, not knowledge." Bertrand Russell.

Silence.

You know, like they say, time is fleeting and so on, sometimes maybe it's better to know. For all of us really it's just a matter of. You know. "Once" was once "soon."

Silence.

Or some people's ideas about the unendingness of the energy of the essence or. Which actually has you know scientific um, a scientific—in that energy cannot be created or destroyed and so on.

Silence.

Of course Tish would just say "Some things just can't be explained." "And that's probably the way it should be." Not that I. Or. Whatever.

RICHARD *(sigh)* Fuck.

SAM Yeah.

RICHARD Can I talk to you?

SAM Sorry?

RICHARD I just need to talk.

SAM Oh sure yeah. Um.

RICHARD It's just I find it difficult to talk to Tish.

SAM Uh huh.

RICHARD And Judy well, she's kind of in her own world you know.

SAM Uh huh.

RICHARD And anyway, they're his sisters... and to talk to them about David and I and our sexual relationship...

Pause.

SAM Uh huh.

RICHARD You see we weren't— *(sigh)* We weren't exclusively together. And we hadn't been for a long time. You know?

SAM Uh.

RICHARD We saw other people.

SAM Oh right of course. No I mean not "of course" I mean.... Sorry. Go on.

RICHARD No it's just—I mean we always saw other people, and I mean maybe that's part of the reason we've stayed together all these years, maybe it was good for the relationship, but see we never talked about it, it was just this unspoken understanding—and I wonder why didn't we talk about it—but I never wanted to talk about it—and I mean David never brought it up and I mean I think about all that and I ask myself, or try to figure out what do I really feel about that, about David, about what's happening now—and when I do that, when I really look at how I feel, I think "Well, irregardless of everything I..."

SAM   Regardless.

RICHARD   What?

SAM   Uh. No. Uh.

RICHARD   What did you say?

SAM   Regardless. You said…. Irregardless isn't a word—

> *Silence.*

Regardless will do.

> *Silence.*

The "ir" kind of makes it a double negative. Which I don't think is what you mean.

RICHARD   A double negative.

SAM   Yeah. Sorry. Go on.

RICHARD   What?

SAM   Do you want to—go on or?

RICHARD   No that's fine.

> *Silence.*

SAM   Oh. Um. I'm going to—get a tea or—Do you want some?

RICHARD   No thanks.

SAM   Excuse me.

> *SAM exits. Silence.*

DAVID (1)   Ottawa.

RICHARD   Ottawa, yes yes yes wherever.

> *Light fades on RICHARD.*
> *Spot fades up on SAM addressing the audience.*

SAM   I um… of course I'm just an in-law here but I uh still I would like to take this moment for David—well if I were going to do something for David—I mean if David had his way we'd probably all be dancing—that's what he loved—he said it was good for the soul. Um. Yes. Um.

Soul. Hm. Words. Words. Problematic. Words trap thoughts. Words are like little cages for thoughts. So you trap the thought in the cage of the word and you look at it and you think: "Well that's not what I was looking for at all" so then you either let it go or make do, and if you do try to make do, well by that time the thought's changed so much all you're really left with is the cage. Problematic. But… David and I had a special way of communicating whenever…. Well not to say I knew David all that terribly well—I didn't, uh don't, never really um. I mean I met Tish and then Tish and I got married, but David was always you know travelling and you know busy and…. Of course he was my best man at our wedding—but that was more Tish's thing—she wanted that—and that was, you know, fine. So, but, yes, okay. Okay. One Christmas we were visiting David, and David and I stayed up after the others went to bed to have a few—well a few more—but um and I mentioned that I could sign the alphabet—which I can because my brother had temporary hearing loss from an accident one summer—he was driving one of those ATV's and it rolled and he ended up hitting his head on—and um right so. And I mentioned that I could sign and David seemed very interested in that and so I taught him how to do it— he actually caught on you know pretty quickly. Um but it became this thing that we had that—I mean it became our own kind of thing—our own little code. Like this for example: *(makes the sign of "B" three times)* which is "B, B, B," which stands for "blah blah blah"—which whenever we were in a room with… someone or other who was going on and on about something or other we would do our "b, b, b" which was you know funny, but also something private, something special, some- thing… you know… nice… and which is interesting because it you know asks the question I mean is this *(gives a thumb's up)* this a word or a signal or a symbol or what—is a word sonic or verbal or mental or…. But anyway that's just… *(He signs "b, b, b.")* Um. Thanks. Sorry. Thanks.

> *Spot fades out on SAM.*
> *Light fades up on TISH, sitting on the bed, holding DAVID (1)'s hand. SAM enters, making notes in his book. TISH fusses with the bed and begins speaking to DAVID (1).*

TISH   You know what I'm going to do?

> *SAM looks up and sees TISH is speaking to DAVID (1).*

I'm going to make some JELL-O. For you and me and Sam. That would be nice eh? *(to SAM)* You'd like some JELL-O wouldn't you Sam?

SAM   Hm?

TISH   Some JELL-O?

SAM   God no. Please no more JELL-O.

TISH *(to DAVID (1))* Then you and I will have some.

SAM Tish I really don't think David's going to be eating any JELL-O.

TISH I know it's just cheery to have around. *(to DAVID (1))* Remember Mom's JELL-O? It took forever to harden because she made it with vodka. And that time we got into Mom's JELL-O and we got lipstick all over her mink coat? Of course it wasn't really mink—she called it mink but it was really beaver or something.

DAVID (1) Ottawa.

TISH *(moving away from DAVID (1))* Ottawa. Yes that was fun wasn't it.

DAVID (1) Matchbook.

TISH Matchbook. *(pause)* Oh my God!

SAM What?

TISH He's remembering those little matchbooks we had made up for our wedding.

SAM Really?

TISH Well sure.

SAM Do you really think our wedding was that important to him?

      Silence.

TISH I guess people don't do matchbooks any more. I wonder what they do now?

SAM Coasters.

TISH Coasters?

SAM When Sidney and Sandra got married they had laminated coasters made with their pictures on them.

TISH Really?

SAM They're splitting up.

TISH I heard.

SAM Lucky we didn't do coasters.

      Silence.

TISH What are you writing?

SAM Nothing.

TISH A little poem?

SAM Notes, nothing.

DAVID (1) German doctor.

SAM What?

TISH "The German doctor", he's been saying it all morning.

> *RICHARD enters.*

SAM Do you know a German doctor?

RICHARD Oh that. I think it's just from a TV program.

SAM Oh right, that show with the German doctor. And that Asian actress. She's good.

RICHARD *(to TISH)* Um…

TISH *(moving to exit)* Excuse me.

RICHARD Listen…

TISH What?

RICHARD Can we call a truce here?

TISH I don't know what you're getting at.

RICHARD Okay, okay. Fine.

TISH Excuse me I'm going to go make some JELL-O.

RICHARD No! No more JELL-O! Nobody wants your fucking JELL-O!

TISH Don't swear at me.

RICHARD I'm sorry.

TISH Who do you think you are?

SAM All right now all righ—

> *Loud bass from next door pounds through the wall.*

TISH *(to RICHARD)* What is that?

RICHARD The guy next d—I'll deal with it.

> *RICHARD exits.*
> *A quick crossfade from the bedroom to DAVID and the STUDENT.*
> *The music grows louder. They shout over the music.*

DAVID —and the Doctor says "Did you know you've got a dozen roses up your ass?" And the fag says "Read the card! Read the card!"

> *The STUDENT doesn't laugh.*

"Read the card!" Get it?

STUDENT I don't like this joke.

DAVID   Why not?

STUDENT   It makes fun of people.

DAVID   Well it's a joke, that's what it's supposed to do.

STUDENT   So I don't like jokes maybe.

DAVID   Oh come on! Lighten up.

STUDENT   No you don't understand.

DAVID   It's just for a laugh.

STUDENT   To me life is a war and it is very important what side you choose to be.

DAVID   Well even in a war they take a break from time to time.

STUDENT   Even when the soldier dreams the war goes on.

> *Silence as the music continues.*

DAVID   So you don't like jokes. What do you like?

STUDENT   I like sex.

DAVID   Sex?

STUDENT   But not here.

DAVID   Uh. No.

STUDENT   I live nearby.

DAVID   Uhhhhhh… I don't know.

STUDENT   Because I don't like your joke?

DAVID   No… because… uh…

STUDENT   The doctor orders.

> *Light snaps out on DAVID and the STUDENT.*
> *Light up in the bedroom. TISH, SAM and JUDY are there as the music continues. Suddenly the music cuts out. After a few moments RICHARD returns.*

RICHARD   That was no problem. If it ever happens and I'm not here just knock on the door. He's very easy-going.

> *Silence.*

JUDY   *(to SAM)* What are you writing?

SAM   Oh just… nothing.

JUDY   What is it?

SAM   It's a little… sort of a haiku.

JUDY   Read it.

TISH   He never reads what he writes.

JUDY   You have to.

SAM   Do I?

JUDY   It doesn't really exist if you don't share it.

RICHARD   Oh please.

JUDY   Read it.

SAM   Well…

JUDY   Read it.

SAM   *(clears throat)* Um. It's a nice little book isn't it.

JUDY   Read it.

> *Silence.*

SAM   Um. Okay. Um. *(reading)* "I asked Why, Why answered not."

> *Pause.*

I should read it again. *(more confident)* "I asked Why, Why answered not."

> *Pause.*

RICHARD   That's it?

SAM   It's a haiku—

RICHARD   It's not a haiku.

TISH   No it's not.

SAM   Yeah it's—

RICHARD   *(reaching for notebook, SAM hangs on to it)* Let me see.

TISH   No it's not.

RICHARD   A haiku has three lines.

TISH   And fourteen syllables.

RICHARD   Sixteen.

TISH   Right. Sixteen syllables.

RICHARD   That's not a haiku.

JUDY   Well it's haiku-like.

TISH   It's short.

RICHARD *(laughing)* It's got that yeah, it's short.

TISH But so's "Pass the salt."

RICHARD "You want fries with that?"

TISH Good haiku!

RICHARD Food haiku!

TISH Haiku Cafe!

> *TISH and RICHARD laugh snortingly.*

SAM Thanks.

JUDY It's nice. It's sad.

SAM Whatever.

JUDY *(looking at the notebook)* And you've personified "Why."

SAM Yeah right—a capital "W." *(to TISH and RICHARD)* It's personification.

> *RICHARD and TISH continue to laugh.*

JUDY The search for reason.

SAM Right.

TISH *(laughing)* Oh spare me.

> *TISH exits.*

RICHARD *(laughing)* I need a drink.

> *RICHARD exits.*

JUDY Guys.

> *SAM and JUDY are alone. He looks down at his book. She looks at SAM. She tweaks his nipple and exits. SAM looks perplexed. Light fades on SAM.*
> *Light fades up in spots on TISH and RICHARD. They stand on either side of the stage, each holding a drink.*

TISH Don't get me started on Judy.

RICHARD Don't get me started on Judy.

TISH Princess Flake.

RICHARD The Queen of The Hemp Parade.

TISH Socialist of the Year.

RICHARD Wouldn't want to go through customs with her, know what I mean?

TISH   You know the type.

RICHARD   And don't get me started on Sam.

TISH   And Sam…

RICHARD   A touch of the poet goes a very long way.

TISH   Poor old Sam.

RICHARD   Makes the Nutty Professor look smooth.

TISH   He just needs a bit of a push.

RICHARD   You know the type.

TISH & RICHARD   And don't get me started on Her Majesty. Her Majesty!

TISH   Oh well doesn't the sun rise and set on Her Majesty.

RICHARD   Doesn't Her Majesty have to run every show.

TISH   The dramatics, really!

RICHARD   And the JELL-O crusade!

TISH & RICHARD   And don't get me started on the carpet.

TISH   The carpet.

RICHARD   The carpet.

TISH   It's a very valuable carpet.

RICHARD   *(mocking)* "It's a very valuable carpet."

TISH   But don't get me started.

TISH & RICHARD   And don't get me started on the wedding.

TISH   The wedding.

RICHARD   The wedding.

TISH   Okay David says to me:

RICHARD   David says to me:

TISH   David says: "About the wedding, Richard's not coming."

RICHARD   David says: "About the wedding, you're not invited." And I think:

TISH & RICHARD   Okay. If that's the way Her Majesty wants it that's the way it's going to be.

TISH   Maybe a family means nothing what do I know.

TISH   But a wedding only happens once—knock on wood—and maybe fine a person doesn't believe in marriage that's a person's prerogative but if nothing else a little common courtesy.

RICHARD   But a wedding is one of those opportunities to forge the family bonds—and fine a person is ignorant and frightened of certain lifestyles but this is family and that's something else.

RICHARD   Family doesn't matter to her that's fine.

TISH & RICHARD   But I guess that's my problem.

TISH   Her Majesty's problem?

RICHARD   Her Majesty's problem?

TISH & RICHARD   A lack of compassion stemming from a basic fear of intimacy.

TISH   See.

RICHARD   Simple.

TISH   You know the type.

RICHARD   But don't get me started.

TISH   And anyway...

RICHARD   this isn't about

TISH & RICHARD   Her Majesty.

RICHARD   And

TISH   this

RICHARD   isn't

TISH   about

RICHARD   me...

TISH   *(a toast)* To...

RICHARD   *(a toast)* To...

TISH   To David.

RICHARD   To David.

Light snaps out on TISH and RICHARD.
Light snaps up on JUDY, she addresses the audience. As she speaks
she peels an orange.

JUDY   Yeah, so. Right. *(mumbling to herself)* Whatever whatever I don't
know whatever. *(sighs, resumes speaking normally)* Yup. 'Kay. Good.
Whatever. I would like to take this moment for David. Of course if
David had his way we'd probably all be dancing. Maybe we should be,
I don't know, maybe that's what should happen now. If there's such
a thing as "should." *(sigh)* David's my brother and he's dying. That's all
I know. That used to make me mad but not anymore, what's the point?
Who am I going to be mad at? It's not your fault. Is it? *(laughs)* I guess
it's just "God's" fault or whatever… whoever… whatever. *(pause)* What
am I supposed to say? It's just more talk, right. See that's something
that me and David liked to do—get away from all the talk. We used to
go out to clubs: Kick It, Jump Club, Domino, Smash—of course none of
them exist anymore either…. But uh…. Yeah we used to go out and
stand there in the middle of the dance floor and it would just be noise
noise noise and you couldn't talk, you couldn't think, you couldn't
even feel anything, except the beat—and that was so cool. And we had
this way of communicating in this weird language we invented—see
I taught David how to do the sign language alphabet—I learned it from
this deaf guy in this welding course I took—and I taught David… well
I tried to teach him but he wasn't catching on too quick… or maybe
I was just a bad teacher—but we worked out this other kinda way of
doing it which would be like *(makes the sign for "p" and points over her
shoulder)* for "gotta pee", and *(makes the sign for "c", the sign for "f" and
covers her ears)* meant "check out the freak on the speaker", and other
stuff, much more nasty, about guys and you know… *(laughs)* like *(makes
the sign for "h" twice then gestures toward her pelvis)* and I won't even tell
you what that means *(laughs)*…. Yeah, anyway… but that was our
special, private, personal thing. Ours. And that was so cool. There's
nobody like David. *(pause)* Anyway whatever that's all.

She throws the orange peel on the floor. She turns toward the bedroom.
Lights go up suddenly on SAM sitting on the bed. She walks toward
the bedroom watching SAM. Through the scene she eats her orange.
Silence.

You're always hiding in here.

SAM   I like it in here. It's peaceful.

JUDY   He said anything?

SAM   "Matchbook."

JUDY   You think it has to do with the matchbooks from your wedding?

SAM   Could be I guess.

JUDY   Doubt it.

SAM   Yeah. Well, who knows?

JUDY   I wonder if he just wants a cigarette.

SAM   Maybe.

JUDY   I wonder what he wants.

SAM   Maybe he doesn't want anything.

JUDY   He must want something or he wouldn't still be alive.

>   *Silence.*

He started going back to church.

SAM   Really.

JUDY   Mmm.

SAM   Well he's a bit of a fatalist—that's pretty Christian. He always believed in reasons for things.

JUDY   I don't.

>   *Silence.*

SAM   Yeah, but it's probably better to believe in reasons for things than not to—don't you think?

JUDY   Why?

SAM   What have you got to lose?

JUDY   Dignity.

SAM   Well dignity's not going to do you a hell of a lot of good when you're dead.

>   *Silence.*

JUDY   Hey. Do you wanna smoke a joint?

SAM   Oh. No. Thanks. Um. Here?

JUDY   Yeah right, Tish'd love that wouldn't she.

>   *She hands SAM a slice of her orange and eats the last slice herself.*

SAM   Yeah, really, yeah.

>   *JUDY holds up her hands, wet and sticky, from the orange. She looks for a place to dry them. She walks up to SAM. She dries her hands in his hair. She pats his hair back into shape and stands with her hands*

> *on his shoulders.*
> *Silence.*

JUDY   I asked Why. Why answered not.

> *JUDY leaves the room.*
> *Light crossfades from the bedroom to DAVID and the STUDENT.*

DAVID   You have a cat.

STUDENT   Pardon?

DAVID   The kitty litter in the bathroom.

STUDENT   Ah yes, no. She ran away.

DAVID   Oh that's too bad.

STUDENT   This happens in life. Things go away when they must.

DAVID   Still it's sad.

> *Pause.*

STUDENT   Will you have some music?

DAVID   Sure. What have you got?

STUDENT   Carole King or ABBA.

DAVID   What?

STUDENT   I have two CDs: Carole King or ABBA.

DAVID   Oh, well, you pick.

STUDENT   You like to be told what to do.

DAVID   *(He raises his hand to his forehead, embarrassed.)* Ummmm...

STUDENT   You have nice hands. You should speak with them.

DAVID   Speak?

STUDENT   I know the alphabet letters of hands. Shall I teach you.

> *Pause.*

DAVID   Sure.

STUDENT   "A."

DAVID   "A."

STUDENT   "B."

DAVID   "B."

STUDENT   "C."

DAVID   "C."

STUDENT "D."

DAVID "D."

STUDENT You are a fast learner.

DAVID I'm good with my hands.

STUDENT Oh, so you're the best man with his hands.

> *Light slowly crossfades from DAVID and the STUDENT to JUDY,*
> *RICHARD, TISH and SAM.*
> *The four stand in separate spots listening to the following tape-*
> *recorded scene, shown in italics (stage directions will be in parentheses*
> *for this section). The tape is authentic; complete with the sounds of*
> *cutlery, people moving about, and so on, and continues, with only one*
> *interruption from JUDY, until the NURSE's appearance.*

GROUP SINGING *...Happy Birthday dear David. Happy Birthday to you.*

> *(Applause etc. on tape.)*

DAVID *God I hate that song. If I have another birthday sing "Stormy Weather"*
or something.

TISH *Oh stop it.*

DAVID *Hey I gotta great joke for you Sam.*

SAM *Oh yeah?*

DAVID *But not in mixed company.*

JUDY *What's that supposed to mean?*

DAVID *I was talking about Richard.*

RICHARD *Ha ha—who wants cake?*

JUDY *Oh man I'm stuffed.*

TISH *It doesn't have nuts in it does it? Sam can't have nuts. Top that up would*
you thanks.

RICHARD *Really? Is it severe?*

TISH *I thought you were going to* *bring somebody, Judy.*	*RICHARD* *A guy I work with* *has that.*
JUDY *Yeah but—*	*SAM* *Uh huh it's, you know,* *common.*
DAVID *Yeah but her* *date didn't* *get out of jail* *in time.*	*RICHARD* *But he's allergic* *to everything* *Even ink—* *and he's a designer.*

JUDY   David.

TISH   You're kidding!

JUDY   He's sweet.

TISH   Jail?!

JUDY   It's not like that.

DAVID   Fraud.

TISH   Oh my God.

JUDY   He didn't do it!

TISH   And what ever
happened to
that pusher you
were dating?

JUDY   He wasn't a pusher!

DAVID   No, they call them
dealers now Tish.

JUDY   It was just grass!

TISH   Well the last
I read it was still illegal. God,
have some sense.

JUDY   Oh and booze is
legal so you don't have a problem.

TISH   What's that
supposed to mean?

JUDY   If the shoe fits sweetheart.

DAVID   Okay girls—

SAM   Whoa.

RICHARD   But of course
it's all on computer now.

SAM   Right right, I guess
that makes it easier.

RICHARD   But I prefer a piece
of paper—a nice
piece of paper.

SAM   Yeah I like paper—
I like a nice piece
of paper.

RICHARD   Yeah there's
something
about it eh?

SAM   And I hate to say
it but this recycled
paper—

RICHARD   No I know.

SAM   It's just not the same.

RICHARD   Not the quality.

SAM   Not like it used to be no.

RICHARD   But whose fault
is that?

SAM   No no exactly exactly.

RICHARD   Is   TISH   Don't start   SAM   Hm?
everything okay?   with me.

TISH   Don't start with me Judy.

SAM   Sort of yeah.

JUDY   Well it's true, that's your second bottle this afternoon.

DAVID   Who's counting?

TISH   I am not going to get angry today Judy.

RICHARD   Did everybody get cake?

JUDY   No you're just going to get drunk.

SAM   What?

DAVID   Boring!

RICHARD   Maybe we should move into the backyard.

TISH   Why do you always do this?

SAM   What?

RICHARD   Did everybody   *SAM*   You okay?
  get cake?

DAVID   All right! Soul Train time!   *TISH*   She's just a brat.

RICHARD   Oh God.   No David.

JUDY   Why do you always condemn my life?

DAVID   Yes! Judy put on something funky—Let's do "The Bus Stop."

RICHARD   David...   *TISH*   I'm not dancing.

DAVID   Yes! It's my birthday and everybody does what I say!

          (*DAVID has a coughing fit.*)

JUDY   Do you want some water?

TISH   Is he okay?

RICHARD   Get him some water.

SAM   Um.

RICHARD   Sit up, sit up.

JUDY   Richard?

SAM   Watch his cake.

RICHARD   Thanks. Here.

          (*DAVID stops coughing.*)

DAVID   I didn't need that lung anyway.

(TISH exits the listening area.)

TISH Are you okay?

(DAVID breathes with difficulty for a few moments.)

DAVID Judy?

(JUDY responds from the listening area.)

JUDY *(aloud)* Yeah?

(on tape) Yeah?

DAVID "The Bus Stop."

TISH Oh God.

SAM Sorry, is this a dance thing?

RICHARD You don't know "The Bus Stop?"

(Disco music starts.)

DAVID All right we're all going to dance—help me up—and then we're all
going to get remarkably drunk and then we're all going to fight some more and
then later I might even smoke a cigarette!

(RICHARD leaves the listening area.)

RICHARD No!

DAVID YES! Because it's my fucking birthday!

TISH David.

DAVID Give it up for me sister!

(JUDY leaves the listening area.

TISH *(squeals with delight)*

SAM Hey is this thing recording?

(Tape stops.)
*Light snaps from the listening area to the bedroom. TISH stands near
the bed watching the NURSE remove the tubing from DAVID (1)'s
chest catheter.*

TISH Is—   **RICHARD** Has—

RICHARD Has he said anything?

NURSE No.

The NURSE exits.

RICHARD Yesterday he kept talking about the squeaky bed.

TISH This bed?

RICHARD   I don't think the bed squeaks.

TISH   I've never heard it squeak.

RICHARD   It's a shitty old bed.

TISH   He's had it forever.

RICHARD   I wanted to get a proper bed. You know, a hospital bed.

TISH   Right right.

RICHARD   He made me promise I'd keep this one.

>   *Pause.*

TISH   It's a shitty old bed but I don't think it squeaks.

RICHARD   He doesn't move enough to make it squeak.

TISH   No I guess not.

>   *Pause.*

RICHARD   But when she sat down before I thought it might have squeaked.

TISH   Or maybe it's the floor.

RICHARD   Oh yeah the floor is terribly squeaky.

TISH   Maybe that's it.

>   *The NURSE re-enters.*

It might be the floor that's squeaking.

NURSE   Okay now we should probably prepare ourselves for—

TISH   But if it's the bed it would be easy enough to fix. Excuse me.

>   *TISH exits.*

NURSE   Okay now, you see how his breathing's gotten very shallow?

RICHARD   Right.

NURSE   And remember how I said before—

RICHARD   Right.

NURSE   So if there are any final preparations—

RICHARD   Okay right.

NURSE   —then now would be the time.

RICHARD   Okay yes.

NURSE   If there's anything I can do…

RICHARD Okay. Thank you. Right.

> *The NURSE exits. RICHARD signs the letter "Y", the letter "O",*
> *the letter "U", and then points to DAVID (1). The light fades to a low*
> *level. RICHARD sits on the bed beside DAVID (1).*
> *Light fades up on TISH addressing the audience. As TISH speaks*
> *JUDY enters and takes up a position at the bed. SAM enters and takes*
> *up a position.*

TISH I would like to take this moment… and I know I've already had
a moment but I don't think there's a limit… ha ha. I was going to have
a little slide show but I didn't really get it together to get it together. Ha
ha. So, I'm um just um going to um talk you through it and you can
imagine the pictures. Okay first there would have been a slide of—
probably there would have been a screen or something here of course—
and um the first slide would be David in the tub—as a baby—a year
or two old or something. And he's smiling and there are bubbles
everywhere and everything and he's smiling. So cute. Um then um one
of David and me—and that would be around David's first day of
school—and you'd see what a little tubby I was—you'd never know it
from looking at me now—well depending on where you were looking
ha ha. And then—the next picture would be our house and then the big
backyard where we used to play with the lake at the bottom—David
called it a lake but it was really a fish pond or something—then—one of
Mom and Dad—Dad's got his sour face on of course and that silly hat
he always wore—you can't really see his eyes there but his eyes were
really lovely—they didn't match the frown at all—and Mom of course
a little tipsy but she was happy she was always pretty much happy—
more or less—unless she wasn't tipsy—then she wasn't very happy at
all. Ha ha. And then a few Christmases and birthdays and so on ha ha.
Then David on his way to his junior prom with his girlfriend Janet—
they were together all through high school—she turned out as it
happens to be a lesbian, but you'd never know it to look at her there
ha ha. Then David's trip to Greece with Judy. That was in—just after he
graduated—I know that because he's wearing the sweater I gave him
when he graduated from college. And um a couple of Judy. Pictures of
David sort of thin out around here because after college he decided he
didn't like pictures—he said he wanted to remember things just as they
were in his memory.

> *Silence.*

And of course our wedding, quite the big "to-do" as you can see.
David's got his nice suit on—he looks a little tired in this picture—well
we all do, that's what weddings are like I guess.

> *Silence.*

This isn't working. What I'll do is—I've got the slides in my suitcase and tomorrow I'll make a couple of calls—I'm sure somebody knows somebody who has a whatchmacallit to actually do it properly. So yes that would be good yes—so tomorrow. Yes.

> *TISH exits. Light fades up in the bedroom. After a few moments TISH enters.*
> *Silence.*
> *JUDY clears her throat.*
> *Silence.*

JUDY It's my carpet.

TISH What?

JUDY Mom gave me that carpet.

TISH Well... I'm not lying.

JUDY No I know... I just had to say that.

TISH Well, have it, I don't care.

RICHARD Was she drunk?

JUDY What?

RICHARD When she gave you the carpet—was she drunk?

JUDY Yeah.   **TISH** Probably.

RICHARD And she was probably drunk when she gave it to David.

> *Silence.*

JUDY Poor old Mom.

TISH Really Judy, you can have it.

JUDY No forget it I'm sorry I said anything.

TISH I'm serious, have it.

JUDY I don't want it.

RICHARD Look, there's no carpet. He sold it.

> *Pause.*

Got ten thousand dollars for it.

> *Pause.*

He went to Europe and spent the whole thing in three weeks.

> *Silence.*

SAM Whoa.

RICHARD   And he didn't even take me.

   Pause.

SAM   I hope he took some pictures.

TISH   David? No.

RICHARD   He hated cameras.

TISH   He never took pictures. Not for years.

   Pause.

JUDY   I didn't know that.

   Silence. The lights shift. A spot on the STUDENT as he enters the space. He watches for someone else to appear on the other side. The four see him from the bedroom.

TISH   Who are you?

STUDENT   Hello.

TISH   What are you doing here?

STUDENT   Hello.

TISH   *(to JUDY)* Is he a friend of yours?

JUDY   I don't think so.

TISH   Who are you?

STUDENT   I'm a friend of David's.

TISH   What accent is that?

SAM   Who is he?

JUDY   Hello.

STUDENT   Hello.

SAM   Who are you?

TISH   He says he's a friend of David's.

SAM   *(to RICHARD)* Do you know him?

RICHARD   No.

TISH   Are you French?

RICHARD   Who is he?

TISH   He says he's a friend of David's.

STUDENT   Yes a friend of David's.

JUDY   Are you German? I think he's German.

SAM   Are you German?

STUDENT   Yes I am from Germany.

JUDY   Did you come all this way?

TISH   How do we know he's telling the truth?

JUDY   Why would he lie?

RICHARD   What's he doing here?

TISH   Ask him something German.

SAM   Uh.... What.... What's the capital of Germany?

STUDENT   Berlin.

SAM   *(to TISH)* Is that right?

RICHARD   How do you know David?

TISH   Say something in German.

STUDENT   What?

TISH   Speak German.

STUDENT   *Warum ist die Bananas krumm?*

SAM   What did he say?

RICHARD   How do you know David?

TISH   Are you a doctor?

JUDY   Does he want to see David?

RICHARD   How do you know David?

TISH   Are you a doctor?

STUDENT   I am nothing.

TISH   Nothing?

STUDENT   I am dead.

DAVID   What's it like?

> *The four turn their attention to DAVID (1) in the bed. The light in the bedroom fades to black.*
> *A spot comes up on DAVID. DAVID faces the STUDENT from across the space.*

What's it like?

STUDENT   To be dead?

DAVID   Yes.

STUDENT   Come and see.

DAVID   No, tell me.

STUDENT   Yes. It is more beautiful than anything you can imagine. It is as if you are the emotion you feel. If you were to love a mountain or an ocean or these things, and the feeling you have in your life when you look at these things? It is as if you are that emotion. You hear a song but not only hearing it but to feel and see and smell it. The notes fly about like soft birds and in other ways it touches your tongue and fills your belly like a wonderful meal. No fear, no worry, not even ideas of these feelings. No more living between "was" and "will be."

> *DAVID sighs.*

And this idea of losing life? Don't be afraid. This is not true. Instead we have our lives back to live again—we begin over but with every answer so we can make it as we wish. Every moment perfect.

DAVID   Really?

> *The STUDENT does not respond.*

Really?

> *DAVID walks toward the STUDENT.*

STUDENT   Ottawa. Apartment. Morning.

> *DAVID stands beside the STUDENT. Light shift.*

Good morning.

DAVID   Hello.

> *A cat mews.*

The cat came back.

STUDENT   Yes. She had her holiday and now she's come home. Back to normal.

> *Silence.*

DAVID   Your bed squeaks.

STUDENT   So do you.

DAVID   What?

STUDENT   What is "squeaks"?

DAVID   It makes noise.

STUDENT   So do you.

DAVID   Oh.

STUDENT   Will you have breakfast?

DAVID   Breakfast? Ah, no I don't eat breakfast.

STUDENT   Breakfast is the most important meal.

DAVID   Anyway, look I should go.

>   *The STUDENT holds up a matchbook for DAVID. DAVID takes it.*

A matchbook?

STUDENT   My telephone is inside. Should you ever need a break from the war.

>   *Silence.*

DAVID   Um. Thanks.

STUDENT   You are the best, man.

>   *DAVID laughs. The STUDENT salutes him. DAVID laughs and gives an exaggerated salute. He turns to leave. The STUDENT disappears.*
>   *Music: the requiem.*
>   *Light up on the bedroom. There is no one in the room. DAVID turns and watches as TISH and JUDY enter and remove the bedding. SAM and RICHARD enter and remove the mattress. The four return and disassemble the bed, removing it from the room. Everything is removed from the room. DAVID steps into the room. TISH enters and stands near him. She looks at the empty room. She breaks down sobbing quietly. JUDY enters. JUDY looks at TISH but cannot comfort her. JUDY exits. After a moment SAM enters. SAM puts his arm around TISH and leads her out as DAVID watches. RICHARD enters and stands near DAVID. DAVID steps toward RICHARD but stops. RICHARD takes a deep breath and approaches the audience. DAVID is still as he watches RICHARD.*
>   *A spot on RICHARD as he addresses the audience.*

RICHARD   I would like to take this moment for David…

>   *Silence.*
>   *RICHARD clears his throat.*
>   *Silence.*

Um.

>   *Silence. RICHARD does not cry.*

Of course if David had his way we'd all be dancing.

>   *RICHARD exits. The music slowly begins to swell. As the music reaches a crescendo DAVID begins to spin. DAVID falls. The music*

continues wildly. DAVID spins again. He falls. He tries to keep spinning. The STUDENT enters the space walking back through it in the opposite direction than he did in the beginning. The STUDENT watches DAVID. DAVID is not aware of the STUDENT but his presence gives him strength. DAVID spins wildly, and spins and spins until it is as if he flies into the air and disappears. The lights to black. The music ends.
Silence.
End.

You Are Here

l to r: David Jansen, Caroline Gillis
photo by Guntar Kravis

You Are Here was developed and first presented at the National Theatre School of Canada, in May 2000, with the following company:

ALISON	Amy Rutherford
RICHARD	Jonathon Ullyot
CONNIE HOY / FIRST AD	Amy Stewart
TED STEEVES	Rowan Tichenor
DOCTOR / WAITER	Jamie Burnett
PHILIP GARAY	Jocelyn Grover
JERRY	Luke Kirby
DIANE DRAKE	Diana Donnelley
TOMAS ROMAN	Rafal Sokolowski
PAUL	Kevin Corey
JUSTIN	Alan Hawco

Special thanks to Alicia Johnston, Maureen LaBonte and Perry Schneiderman.

•

You Are Here was professionally produced by da da kamera (in association with Theatre Passe Muraille) at Theatre Passe Muraille, Toronto, in September 2001, with the following company:

ALISON	Caroline Gillis
RICHARD	Jim Allodi
CONNIE HOY / FIRST AD	Marjorie Chan
TED STEEVES / PHILIP GARAY / DOCTOR / WAITER	Ryan McVittie
JERRY	David Jansen
DIANE DRAKE	Fiona Highet
TOMAS ROMAN	Randy Hughson
PAUL / JUSTIN	Alan Hawco

Directed by Daniel MacIvor
Sound and Music Designed and Composed by Richard Feren
Set and Lighting Design by Andy Moro
Production Management by Lynanne Sparrow
Assistant Stage Management: Lynanne Sparrow
Produced by Sherrie Johnson
Assistant to the Producer: Kimberly Purtell

Characters

ALISON
RICHARD
CONNIE HOY
FIRST ASSISTANT DIRECTOR
TED STEEVES
DOCTOR
WAITER
PHILIP GARAY
JERRY
DIANE DRAKE
TOMAS ROMAN
PAUL
JUSTIN

Notes

I have described *You Are Here* as a one woman show for twelve characters. The main relationship of the show is Alison's relationship with the audience, they are present for her unless she gets lost in the memory of the scene, or when she loses herself in the second act with Justin. The only other people in the play who develop direct relationships with the audience are the other dead people, Richard and Connie Hoy. And yes, Alison is dead.

You Are Here

Act One

A chair sits on the darkened stage. ALISON, unlit but visible, walks out onto the stage. In her hands she holds a clear bottle filled with sand. The house lights slowly fade. She looks out into the audience. She approaches the audience. From the darkness she speaks.

ALISON   Are you?...

A light rises slowly on the chair.

Am I?...

ALISON notices the light on the chair.

Is this for me?

ALISON approaches the chair.

Am I supposed to?...

ALISON sits. She looks out into the audience looking for direction; encouragement; a familiar face. She begins speaking, haltingly at first.

This is my bottle of sand. I thought you might like to see it. It's my one sort of spiritual type possession. It comes from a desert near the Dead Sea. The cradle of civilization. I got it on a trip I took there. Long ago.... Thousands of years ago. Of course not *thousands* literally of course. I guess one should be careful in a place like this, regarding hyperbole and metaphor. You know, what are the rules anyway? I think it's probably best if we just stick to the facts. So.... Yes, long ago, pre-University, late in the last century, I took a bit of a *journey*, to *find myself* back when people used to do that. Do people still do that? I'm sure they do. I've been a little out of touch. Yes, so. I didn't succeed at finding myself on my *journey* but I did find this. The sand. Not the bottle. I mean I did find the bottle but I mean the sand didn't come in the bottle or anything. I mean I put it in the bottle. It wasn't like they had a kiosk or something, selling bottles of Dead Sea sand. But the bottle I got from a shop. Not as an empty bottle. It was full when I got it. It was a local wine. But the bottle of wine wasn't long in my possession before it was an empty bottle. As has always been the case with.... Which perhaps makes the bottle more significant than the sand. Anyway. The thing about it is that it's spiritual, that's important, in that: in here, in this bottle, mixed with this sand is the blood and tears of ancient wars, and the sweat from the building of civilizations, and the very impressions of the footprints of our ancient—perhaps ancestors, searching for the Promised Land. All here in this bottle of sand. (I didn't mean for that to rhyme. That was unintentional.) Anyway. And also, me. I'm in here too, this sand is sand I had been standing upon, which I had been running through my fingers, which mixed my DNA in with all that history. And when I look at this, I feel somehow, that I am part of the larger world; that my life somehow has meaning, that I exist. I mean, I wish I was the kind of person who could find meaning in just sitting down, shutting up and enjoying the beautiful view. But unfortunately, as of yet.... Even growing up I.... But I don't want to talk about growing up. That's not necessary. We've all grown up.... We're all grown up now. Anyway.

She puts down the bottle of sand.

It's just one of those silly things that means something to me. You know how sometimes they ask people "if your house was on fire and you could only rescue one thing what would it be?" Well this would be my one thing. It's not like I would choose it over a cat if I had a cat—in a fire I'd choose the cat of course—I wouldn't choose a bottle of sand over a cat in a fire—if I had a cat—but I never did, have a cat. Or a fire for that matter. Anyway. I wrote something. *(ALISON puts down the bottle and takes a piece of folded paper from her pocket and opens it as she speaks.)* I was trying to think of something pithy—but I've always been too long-winded and too much of a Libra to be pithy. So I thought go for profound—but it becomes apparent quite quickly that the very notion of *going for* profound isn't going to get you anywhere very profound. You just find yourself on this endless, rolling ocean of cliche. *Ocean of cliche.* That's probably the wrong metaphor. Something more ordered. Factory of cliche. "Churning, spinning, something, factory of cliche." Something like that. So too much talk for pithy and no profundity forthcoming I thought I'd keep with the *P* theme and go with poetic.

ALISON reads a few lines to herself.

But you know how sometimes you write something quickly and you don't have a chance to look it over carefully and then when you look at it later it just seems so... written. I've written a lot. For newspapers and magazines. It's how I've made my living. I wouldn't call myself a writer though I've never had that passionate—that kind of passion for writing where I felt, you know "through my veins instead of blood flows ink" or anything like that. Just a job. Celebrity profiles, Who's Hot Who's Not, What Ever Happened To, that sort of thing. No hidden novels or burning ambition.

ALISON sighs.

Maybe passion is the way to go. Maybe passion's what's important. I've always saved my passion for... love. Which is, what is that? Which is, you know, I say love or "I love you" or you know and someone else says: "When you say 'I love you' you build a cage." And maybe they're right. Maybe. It's just language. But some people would say "Language is all we've got to go on." Of course they might contradict themselves later and say "Language is just a vibration in the diaphragm which happens as a result of our response to the idea of the self as an entity separate from the thing we call me." I'm getting too specific. That was always one of my weaknesses as a journalist. That and simply telling the story.

> *ALISON laughs weakly. She considers the piece of paper she still holds in her hand. She puts it away.*

My friend Richard used to say: "The story knows more than you do, let the story tell itself." Which sounds good but.... And anyway I'm not even sure where he got that advice, or more importantly why I should trust it. Knowing Richard. Richard and I met sharing a house in University. I was studying journalism, he was studying social anthropology but his chosen course of study was more *social* than *anthro*.

> *RICHARD speaks from off stage.*

RICHARD   *(offstage)* Alison! Listen to this.

ALISON   Richard?

> *RICHARD appears carrying a notebook and wearing a wildly colourful vest which was the height of style about twenty years ago. He faces out and away from ALISON as he speaks to her. RICHARD reads from the book he carries.*

RICHARD   "The mortal's taste is so fickle, their character so hypocritical, their judgements so wrongheaded, that those persons who pleasantly and blithely indulge their inclinations seem to be very much better off than those who torment themselves with anxiety." Sir Thomas More.

ALISON   *(to the audience)* Richard thought I tormented myself with anxiety.

RICHARD   It's for my book.

ALISON   What book?

RICHARD   My book! My book of quotes.

ALISON   What?

RICHARD   "Live Fast Die Old." My book of quotes I've been working on.

ALISON   Oh that.

RICHARD   Duh. Yeah that. Steeves said he'd help me with it. He said North Americans need any reminders they can get to stop worrying and enjoy life. Steeves gave me this quote.

ALISON   Steeves. *(to the audience)* Ted Steeves. Taught Art History. Wore leather. Screwed his students. Pushed a philosophy of indulgence.

RICHARD   It's not about indulgence. It's about the fact that most people are such high-strung, up-tight, over-achieving assholes that the poor mindless shits who just live and don't get all worked up about it are better off.

ALISON   And who are the poor mindless shits?

RICHARD   The poor mindless shits.

ALISON   Not us?

RICHARD   We should aspire to poor mindless shitdom.

ALISON   *(to the audience)* That was so exactly Steeves. *(to RICHARD)* That is so exactly Steeves.

RICHARD   I thought you liked Steeves.

ALISON   He's a pig.

RICHARD   Since when?

ALISON   Since he's screwing Connie Hoy.

RICHARD   Steeves is screwing Connie Hoy?

ALISON   Yes.

RICHARD   Cool.

ALISON   Connie Hoy is a student.

RICHARD   She's his teaching assistant.

ALISON   She's a student of the University.

RICHARD   She's not his student.

ALISON   She plays dumb and delicate and pretty and sweet.

RICHARD   Uh huh.

ALISON   Connie Hoy grosses me out.

RICHARD   Connie Hoy can gross me out any time.

ALISON   You are such a man.

RICHARD   Is that supposed to be an insult?

ALISON   Yes.

RICHARD   Come on let's go to the party.

ALISON   I'm not going to any party.

RICHARD   Alison!

ALISON   A bunch of hockey players and cheerleaders.

RICHARD   This afternoon you were like "Oh it's going to be a great party, I'm going to wear something sexy."

ALISON   Yeah well it's not this afternoon anymore.

RICHARD   Maybe you'll meet somebody.

ALISON   I don't want to meet somebody.

RICHARD   Come on there'll be lots of nice guys there.

ALISON   What's a *nice guy*? What's *nice*?

RICHARD   I don't know, quiet, smart, you know, fun kind of but not too wild... I don't know, nice.

ALISON   So would you consider yourself a nice guy?

RICHARD   I'm more of, more of, like a dandy.

ALISON   A what?

RICHARD   Or like a cad sort of but in an adorable way.

ALISON   *Nice.* It seems to me that nice is a word used to describe adequate. I'm not interested in adequate.

RICHARD   I don't know. Nice might be amazing. That's what I'm looking for—just a little something nice.

ALISON   Nice is boring.

RICHARD   Look, this is boring. Put on something sexy and lets go. I'll lust after some cheerleaders and you can fall in love some nice guy. Or not. Flirt with some hockey players. Let's just go. Fuck it's Friday night!

ALISON   The time when all good mindless shits go out and indulge their inclinations.

RICHARD   Yeah.

ALISON   No thanks.

RICHARD   At least we can get drunk.

ALISON   (*looking away from RICHARD*) I can get drunk on my own thank you very much.

RICHARD   No fun.

> *RICHARD disappears. ALISON looks after him, a silence in the wake of his absence. After a moment ALISON speaks to the audience.*

ALISON   "Temptations can be got rid of… by giving into them." Balzac. (*She takes another moment.*) Ah, Connie Hoy. I see. I forgot about the book, I forgot about the vest, but Connie Hoy I remember. Oh yes. My Waterloo, my nadir, my bane, my Connie Hoy. It's funny at the time it seemed like it was all about Ted Steeves, but Connie Hoy is the one who stayed with me. Connie Hoy was one of those horrible little creatures who…. But we don't need to get into Connie Hoy. And we certainly don't need to get into Ted Steeves.

> *TED STEEVES appears. A young dapper professor. He speaks out and away from ALISON as RICHARD did.*

TED   Alison?

ALISON   Oh no.

TED   How are you doing?

ALISON   Fine.

TED   Thanks again for dinner.

ALISON   Oh right well no yes thanks.

TED   The pie was delicious.

ALISON   Oh you know.

TED   Anyway. I just wanted to say—

ALISON   Oh that's fine don't worry about it.

TED   Don't worry about what?

ALISON   Whatever it was you were going to say, it's fine.

TED   Oh… kay. How was Richard's trip?

ALISON   Good. Good.

TED   What do people do in Niagara Falls in the winter?

ALISON   Search me.

TED   You haven't been in class this week.

ALISON   I've been you know.

TED   Are you okay?

ALISON   Of course.

CONNIE HOY enters.

CONNIE   Ted? Oh hi Alison.

ALISON   Hi Connie.

CONNIE   *(to TED)* I was waiting. Should I?

TED   No sure I'm just coming now.

ALISON   Bye.

CONNIE   I like your hair, you did something to it.

ALISON   No, it's the same.

CONNIE   *(to ALISON)* How's Richard?

ALISON   Fine fine.

CONNIE   Sharon's been asking about him.

ALISON   He's been you know busy.

CONNIE   I heard he went to Niagara Falls.

ALISON   Yeah.

CONNIE   Crazy guy. Say hi for me.

TED   Me too. And he hasn't been in class lately either.

TED leads CONNIE out. ALISON speaks to the audience.

ALISON   I don't want to get into Ted Steeves.

RICHARD appears carrying a drink.

RICHARD   Steeves!

ALISON   Richard…

RICHARD   Steeves!?

ALISON   Stop it.

RICHARD   Steeves!?

ALISON   Stop it. And what about Connie Hoy anyway. She's just gross.

RICHARD   Why's she gross?

ALISON   She's like one of those girls who goes to nursing school in order to marry a doctor.

RICHARD   A what?

ALISON   She's an embarrassment.

RICHARD   Connie Hoy's going to nursing school?

ALISON   No! God! It's a type thing!

RICHARD   What's wrong with nurses?

ALISON   Richard!

RICHARD   Steeves?!

ALISON   Stop it.

RICHARD   He's so tweedy!

ALISON   He is not.

RICHARD   You had him over for dinner?!

ALISON   Yes.

RICHARD   Steeves!

ALISON   Stop it.

RICHARD   When was this?

ALISON   The night you stayed at Sharon's place.

RICHARD   But you told him I was in Niagara Falls?

ALISON   Yes.

RICHARD   Why didn't you just tell him I was at Sharon's?

ALISON   Because I didn't want him to think you might be coming home.

RICHARD   Niagara Falls?

ALISON   It was the first thing that came into my head.

RICHARD   Because that's where you and Steeves are going on your Honeymoon!!!??

ALISON   Richard grow up.

RICHARD   Steeves!

ALISON   Stop it.

RICHARD   You made him dinner?!

ALISON   Yes.

    A pause.

And a pie.

RICHARD   No!

ALISON   From scratch.

RICHARD   Steeves!

> *RICHARD disappears.*

ALISON   *(to the audience)* It wasn't about Ted Steeves. Yeah yeah, he came over for dinner, I got drunk, I told him I loved him, he didn't know what to say, he waited while I threw up in the bathroom, he kissed me on the forehead and he left. Who doesn't have one of those stories. It wasn't about Ted Steeves. It was about Connie Hoy. Don't let the sweet act fool you. "I like your hair." Yeah right, I like your horns. She was a manipulative, devious, horrible little creature. And she got what I wanted. And it was then, that I promised myself, I'd never get Connie Hoyed again. And having said that—considering the way things are going—I imagine we're about to get the beginning of Jerry.

RICHARD   *(offstage)* Jerry!

> *RICHARD and JERRY enter holding drinks.*

JERRY   How's your dad?

RICHARD   Oh you know.

JERRY   Thank him again for Thanksgiving.

RICHARD   I haven't talked to him since then—he got so on my back, as usual.

JERRY   He just wanted to know if you actually got your degree or not.

RICHARD   Yeah yeah.

JERRY   And I don't even know. Did you?

RICHARD   Yeah no Jerry whatever no yeah no.

JERRY   Okay. It's just you were such an overachiever in high school and now—

RICHARD   I've got a lot on the go.

JERRY   You don't even wear a watch.

RICHARD   I don't like anything on my arms.

JERRY   Yeah but—

RICHARD   Can we move on to another topic? Please?

JERRY   Sure. Um. Have you been to the cottage since—

RICHARD   No no no, a specific topic.

JERRY   What?

RICHARD   You go.

JERRY   Well what?

RICHARD   Specifically something about someone maybe?

JERRY   Someone?

RICHARD   Specifically someone you maybe met recently, at specifically Thanksgiving maybe, at my specifically dad's?

JERRY   Oh Alison!

RICHARD   Bingo. Why don't you ask me some questions about Alison.

JERRY   Okay. Is she seeing anyone?

RICHARD   Excellent question. No she's not.

JERRY   All right. Is she interested in me?

RICHARD   Excellent question. Yes she is.

JERRY   Oh so she knew you were seeing me today and asked that you mention her.

RICHARD   Yes but that's not a question. Keep going.

JERRY   Okay. Um...

RICHARD   What is she doing tonight?

JERRY   Am I asking you that?

RICHARD   Yes you are. Tonight? Well as a matter of fact I'm meeting her later—she just got a job and we're celebrating. Perhaps you'd like to join the celebration?

JERRY   Perhaps. And what does the mysterious Alison do?

RICHARD   Oh the mysterious Alison! The messenger thanks you for such an excellent phrase to return with.

JERRY   Well she was mysterious. She barely said anything about herself.

RICHARD   That's *best behaviour.* Don't get used to that.

JERRY   So you're not interested in her? I thought maybe you and she were...

RICHARD   No! No I know her too well.

JERRY   Is that a negative thing?

RICHARD   It's a friends thing.

JERRY   Have you slept with her?

RICHARD   What?

JERRY   No I mean just have you?

RICHARD   What difference does it make?

JERRY   I'm asking questions.

RICHARD   Well I don't want to answer that question.

JERRY   So you did?

RICHARD   I don't want to ruin your sacrifice to the volcano or whatever you're planning but I don't think she's a virgin Jerry if that's what—

JERRY   I'm asking if you slept with her.

>   *ALISON moves away, looking off, no longer listening.*

RICHARD   Why does it matter?

JERRY   You're my friend.

RICHARD   I think it's pretty weird that it should matter.

JERRY   I just want to know.

RICHARD   Would it make some incredible difference if I did? Would it stop you from pursuing something?

JERRY   It might.

RICHARD   No. I didn't.

JERRY   You did!

RICHARD   No! Jesus! I think Mister Psychiatrist should do a little on himself.

JERRY   I'm a psychologist not a psychiatrist.

RICHARD   Whatever you are take a pill.

>   *RICHARD and JERRY disappear. ALISON speaks to the audience.*

ALISON   Yes. So. Anyway. Let's not talk about Jerry. Let's talk about *Charles.*

>   *PHILIP GARAY appears. Although no youth he is dressed in the up-to-the-minute trend. He flips through a magazine, marking various pages.*

PHILIP   Philip Garay. You're the new girl?

ALISON   Um

PHILIP   Welcome to *Charles.* Do you know why they call *Charles* "The Very Magazine?"

ALISON   Um—

PHILIP   Because it is. Very. Very very. Are you?

ALISON   Am I?

PHILIP   Very very?

ALISON   I…

PHILIP   If you have to think about it you're not.

ALISON   Oh…

PHILIP   You'll be my fifth assistant this year. I'm tough. Do you know how long I've been in this business?

ALISON   Uh…. No.

PHILIP   Good. Have you met the receptionist? She's new too.

ALISON   No I—

PHILIP   If you happen to get friendly with her mention that she should stop tipping her hairdresser. Or maybe she doesn't. Maybe that's the problem. *(re: her dress)* Is that a blend?

ALISON   *(reaching around for the label)* Oh I think it's—

PHILIP   If you have to look it's a blend. Do you work out?

ALISON   I…. No.

PHILIP   Start.

ALISON   Now?

PHILIP   Yes, hit the deck and give me twenty. You're hilarious. Speaking of which, I want you to check out a couple of yoga classes for me.

ALISON   For a story.

PHILIP   No for me. I'm considering getting interested.

ALISON   Uh…. What are you looking for?

PHILIP   A male instructor with a good butt. I always work better with a view. And I like my tea with the bag in. And you have an appointment after lunch.

ALISON   An interview?

PHILIP   My dry cleaning.

    PHILIP disappears.

ALISON   And I made a lot of tea, and I picked up a lot of dry cleaning, and I tried to be nice to each of our many receptionists. And then one day I woke up and realized I had turned into a Connie Hoy. Don't speak up, don't step on anyone's toes, do everything you can to make people like you. A polite little, nice little, little little, Connie Hoy. So that day I went into Philip's office and told him I was sick of being nice to people. And Philip did what only Philip would, and gave me a promotion.

> *DIANE DRAKE appears. A sexy young starlet. She sits, waiting impatiently.*

That didn't mean too much at first other than more responsibility, some perks, nicer restaurants, fewer blends, learning how to play the game, getting good at it, and the opportunity to interview many fascinating and famous people. Fascinating people were always fascinating and famous people were always... well, famous. Diane.

DIANE Pardon me?

ALISON Miss Drake.

DIANE Okay so, first of all I do not want to talk about the clinic. I'm here to talk about the film.

ALISON Fine.

DIANE "Nadia's Body."

ALISON Okay.

DIANE And I don't want to talk about the clinic. It's the story everybody wants but they're not getting it because there is no story.

ALISON Okay.

DIANE And that's all I want to say.

ALISON That's all you want to say?

DIANE About the clinic. Because there's no story.

ALISON Okay. So. "Nadia's Body" was shot in Toronto. Did you enjoy working in Canada?

DIANE Oh Canada is so great.

ALISON And why is that?

DIANE Because it just is. Like people say that Canadians are boring or like prudish or something but they're so not. Everyone is major fun and cute.

ALISON Are you familiar with the concept of the Canadian mosaic versus the American melting pot?

DIANE Uh huh.

ALISON Do you think there's anything to it?

DIANE   Uh huh. Like the way I see things is that I am a very spiritual person. And that ultimately we're all connected.

ALISON   Uh huh… so how do you bring that philosophy to your films?

DIANE   Which films?

ALISON   Any of your films.

DIANE   All my films are so different but I learn so much from each one of them.

>   *A beat.*

ALISON   But "Nadia's Body" is a radical departure from the work you were doing with Tomas Roman.

>   *A beat.*

DIANE   All my films are so different but I learn so much from each one of them.

ALISON   I was wondering how you felt about the nudity.

DIANE   Oh the nudity the nudity, why does everyone want to talk about the nudity? I'm so sick of talking about the nudity.

ALISON   Well you are nude for the entire film.

DIANE   It's called "Nadia's Body"—I'm Nadia and here's her body. Big deal.

ALISON   Okay.

DIANE   It's just like all right… I'm a very sexual person, it's part of me as an actress and of my personality and I think that it's important to use all my parts… *(She laughs.)* of me… of my personality. Right.

ALISON   Will you continue to do work like the edgy work you were doing with Tomas Roman?

DIANE   What do you mean by edgy?

ALISON   Um. Raw.

DIANE   Raw. Cheap you mean.

ALISON   It's about aesthetic.

DIANE   It's about budget.

ALISON   Not only.

DIANE   Only.

ALISON   But a film like Roman's "The Wife Of Hector Finch" doesn't compare to a film like "Nadia's Body."

DIANE   In what way does it not compare.

ALISON   In any way.

DIANE   Well, taste is in the mouth of the you know… taster.

ALISON   It's not about taste.

DIANE   Nobody liked "Hector Finch."

ALISON   It was a wonderful film.

DIANE   Didn't you find it confusing? There were three wives all totally different but all supposed to be the same person. And sometimes we were all in the same scene.

ALISON   It didn't follow a linear narrative line no.

DIANE   It didn't make any sense.

ALISON   Well surely you discussed it with Roman, you were living with him at the time.

DIANE   What magazine do you work for?

ALISON   *Charles.*

DIANE   Is that a tabloid?

ALISON   No it's—

DIANE   Good. Look. Tomas is a lovely guy, but he's got this weird process where you just throw the idea up in the air and everybody runs with it. I don't like that, I like to be told what to do. I don't want to have the idea I just want to borrow it. But that's Tomas, he's an artist. I'm not an artist, I'm an actress.

ALISON   But you have to agree that the scene with the couple on the bridge—

DIANE   I don't have to agree with anything. Look, some people like things they don't understand and some people like to understand things. It's a free world. Anyway. That's probably it, I better get going.

ALISON   When I was doing my research I found something you might be interested in.

DIANE   What?

ALISON   A movie. I watched it. I found it through a Japanese fan club.

DIANE   Which movie?

ALISON   Apparently it's very hard to find. You were working under another name.

DIANE   Oh yeah?

ALISON "Santa's Postman."

DIANE What? "Santa's Postman." Oh my God.

ALISON I'll send the information to your publicist.

DIANE Oh my God! They're unfindable. My mom was in that.

ALISON Yes.

DIANE It was the only movie we ever did together Oh my God.

ALISON You were very cute.

DIANE I was eight. I was so excited—we shot for two months in Greenland. Cold? Gosh! My mom was the Sugar Plum Angel. I had two lines. "It's a very important letter for Santa" and...

ALISON "It looks like there's going to be a Christmas after all."

DIANE Yes!

ALISON And you were right.

DIANE Huh?

ALISON There was a Christmas after all.

DIANE Yeah there was.... And that's the thing see, like I loved my mom so much and when she died I was just so... you know... and I fell in with a bad agency and into the modelling thing and you might as well disfigure your face with a broken bottle as gain a pound right?

ALISON Uh huh.

DIANE Which is I guess how it all started I guess, when I look at it now. That whole thing with the clinic and all that. See it wasn't a drug thing, it was an eating disorder thing.

ALISON But you got through it though, you survived.

DIANE Yeah, I did.

ALISON Your mom would be so proud of you.

DIANE Do you want to keep talking?

ALISON Sure.

> *DIANE rises to leave.*

DIANE I'll just tell my driver. *(turning back)* Thanks.

> *DIANE exits.*

ALISON *(calling after her)* No thank you. Thank you. Thank you for pretending to believe my generosity exceeded beyond the thousand dollars I spent tracking down that stupid movie. *(to the audience)* That was my first feature. It was supposed to be a page sixty-four *What's Up With So and So* type thing. But I got the story everybody wanted and I got bigger desk, and sexier assignments, and a better life, and entry into a world where other people's misfortune was a cause for celebration, where relationships were built on disdain, where air kisses replaced hugs and talent wasn't in the least important as long as you had good tits and a really fabulous pair of shoes. Thanks for that. And most of all thank you for the anger. Because as we all know, anger is a gift.

> *JERRY appears. JERRY speaks to ALISON. ALISON does not look at him.*

JERRY Anger is a gift.

ALISON I know.

JERRY Use your anger. If there's one thing that seems to hold people back it's an inability to use their anger constructively. Your capacity for anger is equal to your ability for action.

ALISON I know.

JERRY Look at me.

> *JERRY approaches ALISON.*

ALISON Why?

JERRY Just look at me.

ALISON Why?

JERRY So I can look at you.

> *JERRY takes ALISON in his arms and turns her to him. ALISON looks at him.*

You're so fantastic.

ALISON I read your story.

JERRY You're so fantastic.

ALISON I liked it. You're a good writer.

JERRY I'm not a writer I'm a psychologist.

ALISON You could be a writer if you wanted to be.

JERRY I wrote that story for you.

ALISON You wrote it before you met me.

JERRY And still I wrote it for you.

ALISON You're such a goof.

JERRY   A goof for you.

> *ALISON moves to leave his embrace.*

ALISON   I should go.

> *JERRY hold her more tightly.*

JERRY   No.

ALISON   *(laughing)* Jerry. I have to get up in the morning. Let me go. What time is it?

JERRY   Guess and I'll let you go.

ALISON   Three… fifteen.

JERRY   Sorry, three-twelve.

ALISON   I was close.

JERRY   Close only counts in horseshoes and hand grenades.

ALISON   And elevators.

> *JERRY laughs.*

JERRY   And elevators. Mmmm.

ALISON   I have to go.

JERRY   Kiss me two more times.

> *ALISON does. JERRY doesn't let her go.*

ALISON   Jerry.

JERRY   Kiss me three more times.

> *ALISON does. JERRY doesn't let her go.*

ALISON   Jerry?

JERRY   Kiss me twelve more times.

ALISON   I have to go.

JERRY   Stay.

ALISON   I'm practically living here.

JERRY   Live here. Move in.

ALISON   Jerry no.

JERRY   You're fantastic.

ALISON   Stop it.

JERRY   You're fantastic.

ALISON   I have to go.

JERRY   No stay and we'll lock the door and unplug the phone and cover the windows with tinfoil so that the sun will never come up and time will pass us by. Time won't ever know we're here.

ALISON   Jerry.

JERRY   Sh! We have to be very very quiet so time won't find us. That way we can just be like this forever. Just like this. Nothing can change from this. From you looking like that and me feeling like this.

A beat. JERRY lets her go and stands behind her.

ALISON   What?

JERRY   Marry me.

JERRY disappears. ALISON speaks to the audience.

ALISON   It's interesting how he said "Marry me." He didn't say "Will you marry me?" or "Let's get married." or "You know I was thinking about it and I thought we might get married. What do you think?" No. He said "Marry me." Like it was a directive. As if I didn't have a choice; "Marry me.", not something we'd do together but something I was supposed to do to him: like "love me" or "feed me" or "burp me." And I never wanted to get married. Ever. Even as a girl. I was never deluded about the romance of a sit-down dinner for seventy-five or a twelve-hundred-dollar prom dress. Or veils. We got past the horse drawn carriage and the trousseau but we never got past the veil? I was never the marrying type. That was Connie Hoy. Who by the way eventually ended up marrying Ted Steeves and having a vanload of kids. But that was Connie Hoy, and I was not Connie Hoy. I was an independent woman and I was going to have an interesting life. Leave marriage to the Connie Hoy's of the world, I never wanted to get married.

RICHARD appears carrying a flower, a drink with ice and a shawl.

RICHARD   Then don't get married.

ALISON   When did you say that?

RICHARD   You let the fire go out.

ALISON   Sorry?

RICHARD   I got it going again. Do you like it here?

ALISON   Here where?

RICHARD   Here on earth.

ALISON   What?

RICHARD   *(laughing)* At the cottage.

> *RICHARD throws the shawl to ALISON, she catches it and puts it on her shoulders. She sits on the floor.*

ALISON   Oh yes, the cottage, I love the cottage.

RICHARD   My dad says he'll give it to me if I get married.

ALISON   That's incentive.

RICHARD   But I don't want the cottage. I'm not going to tell him that though or he might offer me something I want.

> *RICHARD takes a drink.*

ALISON   What do you want?

RICHARD   I want to figure out how to make an ice cube that doesn't melt.

ALISON   Then it wouldn't be an ice cube.

RICHARD   What do you mean? If it's not melting it's not an ice cube?

ALISON   Melting is part of the process of the ice cube.

RICHARD   That's dark.

ALISON   What's dark about it?

RICHARD   You're not enjoying the ice cube.

ALISON   Ice cubes melt, that's their purpose.

RICHARD   No, ice cubes keep things cold, that's their purpose.

ALISON   But they do inevitably melt.

> *RICHARD takes an ice cube from his glass.*

RICHARD   Okay, so this sad little melting ice cube—this is an ice cube?

ALISON   Yes.

RICHARD   But the ice cube in the freezer that's not melting—isn't it still an ice cube?

ALISON   Freezing's just the other side of melting, it's the same thing.

RICHARD   It is not, how can you say that!

ALISON   Anyway it's all just water, ice is what we call the state of frozen water.

RICHARD   You've just negated the existence of the ice cube! That is so dark.

ALISON   Sorry that's life.

RICHARD   With an attitude like that you definitely shouldn't get married.

ALISON   Oh God, why didn't I listen to you.

RICHARD   When I was in Japan I asked Shanti to marry me.

ALISON   The teacher?

RICHARD   No that was Shari, she was English. Shanti was Cambodian. The girl who was helping me with my photography.

ALISON   The prostitute?

RICHARD   Hostess.

ALISON   What did she say?

RICHARD   She said she'd marry me but we'd have to split up when her true love asked for her hand.

ALISON   Where was her true love?

RICHARD   She didn't know, she hadn't met him yet, she just knew he wasn't me.

ALISON   Oh God.

RICHARD   Do you love him?

ALISON   Yes. No. I mean whatever that is. I don't know. Yes. No. I don't know.

RICHARD   I hope you're more decisive about the guest list.

ALISON   Guest lists, invitations, seventy-five people for dinner. I am not wearing a veil.

RICHARD   Do you want to get married?

ALISON   I don't.

RICHARD   Then don't.

ALISON   I mean I do but I don't.

RICHARD   Which is it?

ALISON   It's more the wedding that's bothering me than the marriage.

RICHARD   Then don't have a wedding.

ALISON   What are you saying? Cancel the wedding?

RICHARD   Why not?

ALISON   The invitations have been sent.

RICHARD   The invitations have been sent? Is that reason enough to have a wedding you don't want?

ALISON   Stop it.

ALISON rises, taking off the shawl.

RICHARD   What I say is you should just screw the whole thing and run off with me to Mexico and get married. That's what you should do.

ALISON looks at him. She has heard this line as if for the first time. She does not remember him saying this before. RICHARD looks at ALISON waiting for her to say her next line. A long moment passes. ALISON looks away.

You're supposed to laugh now.

ALISON shoots him a look.

This is the part where you laugh.

ALISON walks past him, dropping the shawl in his lap, then stops facing upstage.

ALISON   Ha.

RICHARD   You'll have to do better than that.

ALISON   HA!

RICHARD   Get married, think of it as a party, have fun.

RICHARD rises, drops the flower on the chair and leaves. ALISON turns, looking after him.

ALISON   Richard…

Now alone ALISON sees the flower lying on the chair. She picks it up and studies it. She sits.

There's a scene near the end of the film *The Wife of Hector Finch* by the director Tomas Roman where Diane Drake as the young wife and the French actor Rene Voltair as Hector Finch run through a park laughing and in love. The wife runs on to a bridge over a river and Hector Finch catches her in his arms. He turns her around and gives her a flower. She smells the flower, she admires it, she smiles, she looks at Hector Finch and then gently rips the flower in half. She holds one half in her hand and gives him the other half. He takes the petals and gently, gently places them in his breast pocket pressing them lovingly into his heart. She takes her half of the flower and throws it into the river laughing. Hector Finch doesn't know whether or not to be hurt but forgets everything as his wife throws herself into his arms and we watch the petals float down the river.

TOMAS ROMAN appears.

TOMAS Yes. And?

ALISON What…. What um…. What did you hope to say with that scene?

TOMAS You're the critic you tell me.

ALISON I'm not a critic I just ask people questions.

TOMAS Perhaps we should talk about "Immediate Action"?

ALISON Sorry?

TOMAS The film we're here to talk about?

ALISON Sorry. Yes. So. How does it feel to be working with Diane Drake again?

TOMAS Wonderful.

ALISON And?

TOMAS What? You want better than wonderful? Or worse?

ALISON Where you hoping to recreate the magic of the "Hector Finch" days by working with her again or…

TOMAS I don't do magic I do movies. Are we here for "Hector Finch" or this film?

ALISON Yes…. Um…

TOMAS "Immediate Action."

ALISON Yes I know um…. And in "Immediate Action" Diane Drake plays…

TOMAS Celeste.

ALISON Celeste. Yes. And the character of Celeste is in almost every scene.

TOMAS Leads usually are yes.

ALISON No of course yes. But I was curious if…. Does your on again off again relationship with Diane Drake in any way hinder… or assist your—

TOMAS Which relationship?

ALISON Your romance.

TOMAS Am I having a romance with Diane Drake?

ALISON According to the press package…

TOMAS   And according to my mother I'm a bum. Let's talk about movies.

ALISON   Okay. Most of your European work remains largely unseen— and now you've taken a very deliberate step into the American mainstream with this more accessible recent work.

TOMAS   This is a question?

ALISON   Sorry. A film like "Immediate Action" seems to be aiming for a different kind of audience—

TOMAS   Aiming? I'm not aiming at anything. Let's move on.

ALISON   It's clear you are a very gifted filmmaker and yet the American producers you've been—

TOMAS   Do you believe in God?

ALISON   In...

TOMAS   Do you?

ALISON   Not in a conventional sense.

TOMAS   So no?

ALISON   So.... No.

TOMAS   And when you say I'm gifted, from whence does this gift come?

ALISON   Chance? I don't know.

TOMAS   In my work I'm embracing my own confusion, my own insignificance. There's no gift there is only insignificance.

ALISON   But your earlier films...

TOMAS   You critics! You critics! What is it you critics want!?

ALISON   I'm not a critic I just—

TOMAS   My early films! My early films! Let it go, they're gone, they were naive, they were simplistic, they were sentimental. No one wants to see these films! I have a house in Italy for my mother I have a house in France for an ex-wife and two children, I have a shack in Mexico for myself! I pay tax in three countries! I have to make money! I can't make these stupid films you people want to see! For God's sake you people!

   A beat. ALISON begins to weep.

ALISON   I'm sorry.

TOMAS   Oh my God this is insane.

ALISON   I'm sorry.

TOMAS   Stop that now. Stop.

ALISON   Yes I'm sorry. Do you have a—

> *TOMAS produces a handkerchief.*

Thank you.

TOMAS   I'm sorry I upset you.

ALISON   No, I'm sorry. I don't know what's wrong with me.

TOMAS   I just can't keep reading these stories of how I was so promising and now I'm so crap. Another story of my artistic decline.

ALISON   No that's not what—I'm a fan. Really. "Hector Finch" was such a beautiful film. And that scene on the bridge—it really spoke to me— it really made me feel something. Maybe that's what's wrong. I don't know. I got married recently and...

TOMAS   I see.

ALISON   No but everything's fine. It's fine. But when I think about that scene... how you really nailed the paradox—how we think we're supposed to keep the flower but really it's better if we throw the flower away. And not just the paradox of relationships but the paradox of life.

TOMAS   If you like.

ALISON   I'm sorry, I'm being ridiculous.

TOMAS   It's a frightening thing. To throw the flower away. It goes against all our instincts. We want to keep the flower, to own it. We want to own it all, the flower, the sunset, the lover, the air we breathe. And with everything we own we become bigger and bigger. But so big, then we realize, inside all that big is so much space to feel empty. Better to face the truth and know we own nothing, we can only own nothing, and better that we should. *(a moment)* This is nice. Nice to have some feeling in the room for a change. But of course this is just me getting old and you having a bad day.

ALISON   The strange thing is I'm not really having a bad day.

TOMAS   This is a good day?

> *ALISON laughs.*

You know, for what it's worth? If I could see one good script? For nothing! I would do it for nothing. I see these scripts and oh my God! But this is what they pay me for. But producers are idiots, anyone can produce you just have to be organized and know how to use a telephone. No but, the other way. Telephone first. Organized is negotiable.

> *ALISON laughs.*

So we call the interview over?

ALISON   Yes fine.

TOMAS   Good. So now can I take you out? To dinner.

ALISON   Take me out?

TOMAS   Sure.

ALISON   I don't think so.

TOMAS   You're very beautiful.

ALISON   I'm very married.

TOMAS   I'm very hungry.

> *ALISON laughs.*

Shall I make the reservation?

> *A beat. ALISON revels in a moment of nostalgia.*

What is it?

ALISON   Nothing.

> *ALISON hands the flower to TOMAS.*

Maybe some other time.

> *TOMAS leaves. ALISON's DOCTOR appears carrying a folder.*

DOCTOR   Alison?

ALISON   Yes?

DOCTOR   I guess you came in for your test results.

ALISON   Sure.

DOCTOR   Not too much to report really—Oh yes, just a little thing. I do get a sense of why you've been so emotional lately.

ALISON   Yes. Right. Yes.

DOCTOR   You're pregnant.

ALISON   Yes I am.

DOCTOR   Yes you are.

ALISON   Yes I am.

DOCTOR   Congratulations.

ALISON   *(to the audience)* And yes and congratulations and yes. And it was like a door opened on a room I didn't even know I had. A room with a beautiful view. For the first time. For a little while I understood everything—things made sense. Just my body even—just The Human Body suddenly, finally made sense to me. Things worked.

> *ALISON sees something across and just offstage. She rises and moves toward it. To the audience.*

What's this? What's this for? Is this for me?

> *ALISON reaches just offstage and picks up a glass tumbler containing a deep red liquid.*

What day is this? Wait. No. Is this that Monday? Is this that Monday morning? Don't I get a choice?

> *JERRY enters and sits reading a newspaper.*

JERRY   Good morning.

ALISON   Good morning.

JERRY   What's that?

ALISON   I made you some beet juice.

JERRY   I'm on a fast.

ALISON   You can drink juice on a fast.

JERRY   No thanks.

ALISON   I didn't sleep at all last night.

JERRY   Was he moving around a lot?

ALISON   No *she* wasn't.

JERRY   I just don't want to say *it*.

ALISON   Why always *he*? Why never *she*?

JERRY   I don't know why we just didn't go ahead and let them tell us at the ultrasound and avoid all this.

ALISON   Avoid all this what?

JERRY   This banal banter.

ALISON   Sorry. I'll try and be more stimulating.

JERRY   Good morning darling.

ALISON   Good morning darling.

JERRY   I'm sorry you didn't sleep well.

ALISON   If somebody told me I was going to end up in a relationship where we called one another darling I would never have believed it.

JERRY   Well what would you like me to call you? Dear? Honey? Baby? Sweetie? Fuckbucket?

ALISON   Fuckbucket. Yeah call me fuckbucket.

JERRY   That's funny: "end up." That's funny.

ALISON   End up what?

JERRY   You said you never thought you'd "end up" in a relationship where you said darling. What is this "end up?" Have we *ended up*? Is this the end of something? What's ended?

ALISON   It's just a figure of speech, don't analyze everything to death.

JERRY   It's language. It's all we've got to go on. Fuckbucket.

ALISON   No, there's also action. And as the saying goes action speaks louder.

JERRY   The importance of action does not negate the importance of language…. God I hate when you do that.

ALISON   Do what?

JERRY   These broad…. These eliminative comparisons.

ALISON   Sorry? "Eliminative?" I pity your poor patients.

JERRY   Ha!

ALISON   What?

JERRY   Pity away. My patience. My poor patience. My challenged virtue.

ALISON   Once upon a time I would have found that cute, now I just want to hit you on the head with a waffle iron.

JERRY   We don't have a waffle iron.

ALISON   Lucky for you.

JERRY   I'll count it among my blessings.

ALISON   Everything's an argument, everything's an argument, everything's an argument.

JERRY   Would you like me to argue that?

ALISON   Say "I love you."

JERRY   Alison.

ALISON   Say it.

JERRY   When we say "I love you" we build a cage.

ALISON   You used to say it.

JERRY   I used to build cages.

   ALISON sighs.

   You know how I feel.

ALISON   Drink your juice.

JERRY   Did you read the new draft?

ALISON   Of?

JERRY   Of the screenplay.

ALISON   Oh. I didn't yet no.

JERRY   I thought you were going to show it to some people. Or—don't feel obligated. I mean if you think it has potential. But if it's no good just be honest.

ALISON   It's good.

JERRY   If you don't want to show it to anybody—

ALISON   —I will—

JERRY   —I mean why not explore connections you know—

ALISON   —I know—

JERRY   —If it's any good—

ALISON   —It is—

JERRY   Or...

ALISON   I will. Drink your juice.

JERRY   I don't like beet juice.

ALISON   You're not supposed to like beet juice you're supposed to like scotch.

JERRY   I'm on a fast.

ALISON   It's good for you.

JERRY   I'm on a fast!

ALISON   Are you having an affair?

JERRY   I thought we were talking about beet juice.

ALISON   I know but are you?

JERRY   God Alison. Your hormones must be...

ALISON   Are you?

JERRY   With whom?

ALISON   I don't know…. Some woman you met somewhere…. Some patient.

JERRY   Yes I'm having an affair with a patient. I was going to wait until she got off crack and broke things off with her pimp before I told you about it. Jesus Alison.

ALISON   I'm sorry.

JERRY   I love you okay?

ALISON   Oh don't say it like that.

JERRY   Like what?

ALISON   You're just saying it because I'm an idiot.

JERRY   You're not an idiot.

ALISON   I don't know what's wrong with me.

JERRY   You're pregnant it's normal.

ALISON   Is it?

JERRY   Yes.

ALISON   Oh God. I'm sorry. I think I'm close to losing my mind.

JERRY   I wouldn't worry about it. *(beat)* Close only counts in horseshoes and hand-grenades.

ALISON   And elevators.

JERRY   Have a nap. I'll call you later.

ALISON   Okay. Yeah. I'll be better later.

JERRY   Bye.

> *JERRY leaves.*

ALISON   Bye.

> *ALISON watches him go. She looks out at the audience.*

And I remember this was Monday because it was the first day of the twenty-first week. I counted in weeks because nine months seemed so much longer than forty weeks. Forty Mondays and this was twenty-one. The twenty-first week, the twenty-first Monday.

> *ALISON slowly pours the beet juice onto the ground as she speaks.*

After twenty-one comes…. Eighteen, nineteen, twenty, twenty-one. Twenty-one. Twenty-one. Eighteen, nineteen, twenty, twenty-one. After twenty-one. Twenty-one. After twenty-one we stop. We stop counting after twenty-one.

RICHARD appears. Silence.

RICHARD   It's nice out. It's almost hot. But not in a bad way.

A beat.

Apparently it's warmer than it's been for ages. For this time of year. It's a record or something. I mean it should be, you know, much colder.

A beat.

I'm not complaining.

A beat.

Hey, I haven't had a cigarette in three days! How about that? It's not even that hard. They say after three days all the nicotine is out of your system. Maybe this is as bad as it gets. Right? Maybe? Don't count on it. Right?

A beat.

But it's working. I've got a method this time. The No Method Method. No patches, no hypnotism, no nothing, just cold turkey. Which is a very specific kind of mindset. I was thinking I could get a kind of package together and start doing seminars. Cause it's working for me, it could work for other people right?

A beat.

You set your mind to it. You change yourself or whatever.

A beat.

I'm not eating more either. I'm just not really sure what to do with my hands. They say you're supposed to start doing something. To replace the smoking? A hobby or something. Maybe I should take up stamp collecting. Or ship building. Or bowling. Ha ha bowling. Didn't we used to go bowling? A few times. In University. Get high and go bowling or something.

ALISON   What's it like out?

RICHARD   What?

ALISON   What's it like out?

RICHARD   It's nice.

ALISON   I hate that word.

RICHARD   It's pleasant.

ALISON   I'm so tired.

RICHARD   Should I go?

ALISON When I was a kid—after my dad left, sometimes my mom would get so drunk my aunt would take me for a few days. My aunt lived in the suburbs, and as a treat what she'd do is take me to one of those big malls—with the pastel people and the plastic food places and the stores for everything and escalators for days. And what I used to do was go up to those big maps—those illuminated floor plans that had the little green dot that told you where you were. And I would stand there and stare at the little green dot that was supposed to be me, where I was, and I would get this... be filled with this sense of.... That someone was watching, that someone was in charge. And if someone was watching, if someone was in charge, then maybe whoever they were might understand how I felt. But there isn't. And they don't.

RICHARD I understand how you feel.

ALISON How do I feel?

RICHARD Filled with rage. So tired you can't lift your head off the pillow but filled with rage. Like what quicksand feels like. What it feels like to be quicksand. Big and angry and deep and empty. Like if someone stood over you they'd sink down and never get out.

ALISON looks at RICHARD.

But you'll feel better later. You will.

ALISON Then why can't it be later? Why does it have to be now? Why do we have to be here?

RICHARD We don't.

RICHARD turns and addresses the audience.

We're going to take a little break now.

The house lights slowly come up as RICHARD exits.

ALISON *(calling after RICHARD)* Richard! Thank you. *(to the audience)* Let's have a little break. Everything's going to be okay. Let's all have a break, have a drink. *(exiting)* I'll see you in a little while. Everything's going to be fine. Do you think I could have a drink, just a little—a glass of—

ALISON is gone. The stage is empty.

End of Act One.

Act Two

LIGHTS fade up. Several moments pass. ALISON finally enters laughing. She is drinking a glass of wine.

ALISON Don't believe what you hear about time when people say that time is against us because time is in fact, yes, our friend. Time passes and with it takes everything. And we start over, it's all new again, the first time, we can forget, we can feel better, we can be in love again, anything. It's going to work this time. From here on. It is. Everything's going to be great. It really is. Come on, let's go somewhere. Let's get out of here and go somewhere and do something fun. Let's just go out and get drunk or something.

JERRY appears.

JERRY Getting drunk's not that much fun.

ALISON Let's go out.

JERRY I can't. I can't see people. It just reminds me how stuck I am. I'm so stuck.

ALISON Jerry you're not. How?

JERRY Every day I see my clients…. Clients, that's a joke! It implies I perform some service. Every day, I see them, I talk to them and they're not going to get any better. They're not. And that's supposed to be okay. That's how the system works. I'm working maintenance. I'm a maintenance man. I might as well be working in a fucking factory.

ALISON I read the new draft. I read it this morning.

JERRY Whatever.

ALISON It's going to be something Jerry, we're going to do it right.

JERRY It's stupid to even think we can do this.

ALISON Jerry? "A long journey starts with a single step."

JERRY For Christ's sake Alison.

ALISON Jerry? Look at me. Jerry? We'll be happy. We'll get what we want and we'll be happy.

JERRY I…

ALISON Jerry? You want to make this movie?

JERRY It's ridiculous.

ALISON Jerry?

JERRY   Yes.

ALISON   Would that make you happy?

JERRY   Yes.

ALISON   I'll make you happy.

     JERRY disappears while TOMAS appears. He is holding a script.

So you've read the script?

TOMAS   Yes, thank you.

     TOMAS hands the script to ALISON. A beat. She takes it.

ALISON   He's working on another draft right now.

TOMAS   Is that an apology or a warning?

ALISON   Pardon me?

TOMAS   He does what your husband?

ALISON   He's a psychologist at a hospital, he has mostly outpatients; a lot of people with drug problems, criminal records. The Clayton character is a composite of a few of the people he's worked with.

     ALISON approaches TOMAS and opens the script for him, flipping through it, looking for a scene, eventually handing it off to him.

I think it's good. The characters are very real. Sondra needs a little work but she's coming along nicely in the new draft. The weakness really is in the structure but that's fixable.

TOMAS   Everything is fixable.

ALISON   At the same time there's something fresh about the flawed structure.

TOMAS   Everything is fixable.

     TOMAS hands the script back to ALISON. A beat. She takes it.

ALISON   For Clayton I'm thinking an unknown—someone maybe without a lot of training. Someone real. Which means for Sondra we'd need a name.

TOMAS   Mmm.

ALISON   What do you think of the title?

TOMAS   What is it called again?

ALISON   "The Centre of the Universe."

TOMAS   I don't know. Pretentious certainly.

ALISON   It's Clayton's perspective.

TOMAS   Mmm.

ALISON   So what do you think?

TOMAS   About what?

ALISON   The script.

TOMAS   Very North American.

ALISON   In what way?

TOMAS   In the way that it is exclusively concerned with itself but rationalizes its self-centeredness as an expression of the familiar; as *sharing*. It fundamentally lacks the conviction of its own self involvement.

ALISON   Oh. Where do you see that?

TOMAS takes the script from ALISON and flips through it.

TOMAS   Scene 2. Scene 3. Scene 7. Scene 15. Scene 16. Scene 20. Scene 21. Scene—

ALISON moves to take the script.

ALISON   Fine.

TOMAS walks away with the script

TOMAS   For example. In Scene 22, in the graveyard, Clayton spends an entire page detailing the events of his life for Sondra and when she says: "What a remarkable life." Clayton responds: "But just a life like any life." What is this? If it's no different than any life then why waste my time with it? If it's already my life then there's nothing to tell me.

ALISON   But he goes on to say…. But…. Clayton's just—Jerry's just pointing out—We can all identify with his struggle.

TOMAS   Bullshit. Jerry's saying: "But just a life like any life."

ALISON   I'm sure he's not married to the line, he can change it.

TOMAS   It is not the line! It is the mind behind the line. This…. This… feigned belief in universality. This mortal fear of exclusivity. Bullshit. What is interesting, what is dramatic is *I* and *Now* not how alike we are and how this has always been the way. No particular offense to your husband, this is the problem with most screenwriting these days.

ALISON   I guess that explains it then.

TOMAS   What?

ALISON   Why you haven't made a film in five years.

ALISON takes the script from TOMAS.

TOMAS Who are you talking to about producing?

ALISON I'm producing.

TOMAS You?

ALISON I want to see this film get made.

TOMAS There's more to it than that.

ALISON And I'm organized and I can use a telephone.

TOMAS But we're not joking now.

ALISON And I am owed many favours by many people.

TOMAS Are you trying to save your marriage?

ALISON Pardon me?

TOMAS I just wonder—Such a sacrifice?

ALISON I want to make something.

TOMAS For your husband?

ALISON And myself.

TOMAS All right. Let's set up a meeting with the writer.

ALISON He'll have the new draft by Friday.

TOMAS Good.

ALISON But…. And…

TOMAS Yes?

ALISON Can you get Diane Drake?

TOMAS Ah, perhaps there is a producer in there.

TOMAS disappears. The FIRST Assistant Director enters wearing a headset and carrying a script. As she passes ALISON she hands ALISON the script and takes ALISON's glass of wine. As the FIRST AD takes ALISON's wine, ALISON reaches to keep it and in the process drops the script which scatters across the floor. Through the scene ALISON scrambles to gather the pages.

FIRST AD *(in to headset)* Apparently she left the hotel… I don't know when…. They're lit…. Yes they're lit now…. We could go to an exterior…. It's not my call…. That's a producer call…. Yes there is…. Right in front of me…. What?… I'm losing you…. Hello? Hello?… *(exiting)* Batteries!

PAUL enters wearing a makeup apron and carrying a script.

PAUL   Alison? I've got some problems with this scene.

ALISON   Which scene, Paul?

PAUL   The one with Clayton in the church with the prostitute.

> *DIANE DRAKE crosses the stage.*

DIANE   Morning.

ALISON   Diane the call was for eight-thirty.

DIANE   I told Jennie I'd be late.

> *DIANE exits. The FIRST AD crosses the stage rushing after DIANE.*

ALISON   Who's Jennie?

PAUL   64A.

ALISON   Who's Jennie?

FIRST AD   Assistant wardrobe.

ALISON   She called the wardrobe assistant to tell her she'd be late?

> *The FIRST AD exits.*

PAUL   Scene 64A.

ALISON   What?

PAUL   64A with Clayton and the prostitute in the church?

ALISON   Right okay what?

PAUL   Does it have to be in a church?

ALISON   Yes. That's the location.

PAUL   I don't want to be disrespectful.

ALISON   Pardon me?

PAUL   Can't it be in a park or something.

ALISON   In a park.

PAUL   Instead of a church. I don't want to be disrespectful.

ALISON   To whom?

PAUL   To God.

ALISON   God doesn't care.

> *The FIRST AD enters.*

FIRST AD   Hair says this day has already been established but that's not what I've got in my notes.

PAUL   God cares.

ALISON   *(to FIRST AD)* What day is it?

FIRST AD   Day 13. Church and exterior.

PAUL   We could do it outside the church even.

ALISON   *(to FIRST AD)* What do Hair's notes say?

FIRST AD   Hair doesn't have his notes.

ALISON   Then how does Hair know?

FIRST AD   That's what I said!

> *The FIRST AD exits.*

PAUL   I wouldn't mind if it was outside the church.

ALISON   Paul there are twenty-five people in the church right now who have been lighting it for the last three hours.

PAUL   It's just I prayed on it last night and I don't have a good feeling about it.

ALISON   The scene was always set in a church Paul.

PAUL   I only prayed on it last night.

ALISON   Maybe you should have prayed on it before.

PAUL   I'm just trying to tell you how I feel.

> *The FIRST AD enters.*

FIRST AD   Hair says he needs two hours with Diane.

ALISON   Well tell Hair…. For Christ's sake!

> *The FIRST AD exits.*

PAUL   Do you pray Alison?

ALISON   Not lately.

PAUL   It doesn't matter what you believe. You can still pray. It's just about taking a quiet moment to consider what's important. Maybe we should pray together right now.

ALISON   Fuck off Paul. Please.

PAUL   I don't have a good feeling about this Alison.

> *PAUL exits. TOMAS enters.*

TOMAS   We're lit. The light itself is lit. Can we get something happening here?

ALISON   Diane just arrived and apparently Hair needs two hours with her which can't happen but I can't talk to Hair because Hair won't talk to me because apparently I'm shrill with him and now Paul has some kind of spiritual crisis about getting a blow job in a church.

TOMAS   Ah, it was ridiculous to set that scene in a church.

ALISON   What?

TOMAS   Another bald metaphor.

ALISON   Well.... But the church is lit.

PAUL enters.

PAUL   Oh hey Tomas, listen I want to talk to you about this scene.

TOMAS   In the church?

PAUL   Yeah, see I'm a Christian and—

TOMAS   Yeah I know.

PAUL   Oh yeah?

TOMAS   Yes it's why you were cast in the role.

PAUL   Oh.

TOMAS   And this scene.... What number is this scene?

PAUL   64.

TOMAS   64.

PAUL   64A.

TOMAS   And how many scenes in the script.

PAUL   Uh...

TOMAS   One hundred and twenty two. This scene 64, at the almost exact centre of the script—of the story—to remind us that God is at the centre of life—at the centre of the universe.

PAUL   Oh.

TOMAS   Good writing huh? When it knows more than we do.

PAUL   Yeah.

TOMAS   Bye bye.

PAUL   Bye.

TOMAS   Bye bye.

TOMAS sends PAUL on his way.

ALISON   *(to TOMAS)* Thanks.

TOMAS   And you are shrill with Hair.

ALISON   I know.

TOMAS   In my many years in film you know the one thing I've learned? A few flowers never hurt a hairdresser.

ALISON   Okay.

TOMAS   Looks to me you could use a few flowers yourself.

> *JERRY enters holding a doughnut. As ALISON talks to JERRY she manages to gather up the last of the script pages.*

JERRY   Hey!

ALISON   Hi.

TOMAS   *(to JERRY)* We need to talk about the script.

JERRY   Is there a problem?

TOMAS   *(exiting)* We need to talk about the script.

JERRY   *(to ALISON)* Again?

ALISON   Oh he's a director, directors always want to talk about the script.

JERRY   How's it going?

ALISON   Great!

JERRY   It's really exciting isn't it.

ALISON   Yeah.

JERRY   Listen I'm sure you're really busy but I was just at the food table thing?

ALISON   Craft services.

JERRY   Yeah, and the doughnuts were really stale.

ALISON   Oh. Okay. Well I'll get somebody to get somebody on that.

JERRY   It would probably be a good thing. For morale you know.

ALISON   Morale yes morale.

JERRY   See you later.

ALISON   See you later.

> *JERRY gives ALISON the doughnut and leaves. The FIRST AD crosses and takes ALISON's script. ALISON throws the doughnut after JERRY.*

RICHARD   It doesn't matter what you do it's going to happen the same way.

ALISON   What?

RICHARD throws a sweater at ALISON.

RICHARD   You still haven't learned to start a fire.

ALISON   There was nothing to burn.

RICHARD   There's two full cords of wood out back.

ALISON   I'd like to burn that goddamn film is what I'd like to burn.

RICHARD   You're getting ahead of yourself.

ALISON   What?

RICHARD   Some people liked the film.

ALISON   Who liked it?

RICHARD   Jerry says it's going to do well on video.

ALISON   Yeah in Thailand.

RICHARD   What's wrong with Thailand?

ALISON   Nothing forget it.

RICHARD   It's too bad Jerry couldn't come up this weekend.

ALISON   I didn't invite him. He's busy. He got a couple of story editing jobs.

RICHARD   See that's good. The movie got him some connections.

ALISON   Uh huh.

RICHARD   Connections. That's what it's all about. Before my dad died he was always on me about making connections he was right. He was right but he was wrong.

ALISON watches RICHARD. She hears him in a way she hasn't heard him before.

Because it's not just the networking kind of connections. It's the connections of everyone—of all things—you know? And I was thinking: I don't really feel very connected to anything really. Sometimes lately when I'm here at the cottage I feel like *I like it here* but I think a feeling of connectedness is supposed to be more than just *I like it*. Do you know about Atman? It's a Hindu thing. It's the eternal part of us that is beyond physical description. It's like, something about *that which pervades all*. Something about being the thing and being the thing which experiences the thing and the thing that understands that experience all at the same time. It's pretty interesting. I'm thinking about getting into Hinduism.

ALISON   That might be good for you.

RICHARD does not hear ALISON because this is not the way she answered him when they originally had this conversation. He repeats himself until she says the line she said.

RICHARD   I'm thinking about getting into Hinduism.

ALISON   That might be a good thing for you to do.

RICHARD   I'm thinking about getting into Hinduism.

ALISON   I think it's a good idea to try something different.

RICHARD   I'm thinking about getting into Hinduism.

A beat.

ALISON   You'd never stick to it, you never stick to anything.

RICHARD   That's true.

ALISON gazes out into the audience through the remainder of the scene.

Do you want to sit outside?

ALISON   Not right now.

RICHARD   We'll take our drinks, I'll roll a joint, we'll sit on the porch.

ALISON   Not right now.

RICHARD   It's nice out.

ALISON   Fuck nice.

DIANE DRAKE enters drinking a glass of water and reading aloud from a magazine. ALISON sits silently looking away from the action.

DIANE   *(reading)* "As a film 'The Centre of the Universe' owes more of a debt to Russ Meyer than Scorcese or DePalma..." Who's Russ Meyer?

RICHARD   Isn't he a British guy or?... Alison?

DIANE   Anyway. *(reading)* "The film sloshes along with former art house darling Tomas Roman at the rickety helm..." The helm.... That's a ship thing isn't it.

RICHARD   Yeah I think so. Yeah it is.

DIANE   Ship metaphors are so boring. Blah blah blah.

JERRY enters with a bottle of wine and a glass for himself and one for RICHARD.

JERRY   *(to ALISON)* Do you want the salad dressed now?

DIANE   Who's Russ Meyer?

JERRY   An American director from the 60s and 70s.

DIANE   Is he good?

JERRY   He was a master of a certain kind of cinema.

>   *JERRY hands RICHARD a glass and pours him some wine.*

DIANE   Well that's good!

RICHARD   It's a recommended rental. They gave it a recommended rental.

JERRY   They said it was unintentionally hilarious.

RICHARD   But they recommended it.

JERRY   *(to ALISON)* Salad's done, you want it dressed?

>   *ALISON does not respond.*

DIANE   No you see Robert the thing is—

RICHARD   Richard.

DIANE   What did I say?

RICHARD   Robert.

DIANE   No no I meant to say…

RICHARD   Richard.

DIANE   Yeah. No the thing about the film is it didn't work because it was too real and the people who needed to see it didn't see it because the people who did see it were too afraid of how real it was.

RICHARD   Uh huh. Yeah I kind of get that.

DIANE   Because the people who did see it were the goddamn critics. But here's to the life "The Centre of the Universe" deserves—which it will have now on video—because the people who need to see it will see it— unless the goddamn critics get in the way again. But more importantly here's to Jerry and many more future projects.

RICHARD   Here here. Cheers.

DIANE   Cheers. *(to JERRY)* You really must write something else for me. Just something small. *(to RICHARD)* He's such a wonderful writer—it's such a pleasure to speak his words.

RICHARD   *(to JERRY)* Whoa. Hey.

DIANE   *(to JERRY)* Cheers.

JERRY   Cheers.

RICHARD   *(to DIANE)* So you're in town for awhile?

DIANE   I just came in for the video launch and some meetings—and I have a Naturopath here I like.

RICHARD   But you know I must say Diane you were great in the movie.

DIANE   Ahh you're sweet. Thanks it was fun. Too bad about that little fellow, what was his name?

JERRY   Paul?

DIANE   Paul yeah, he was sweet but—not much presence really though did he.

ALISON   Some people thought he carried the movie.

DIANE   Carried it?

ALISON   Yes.

DIANE   *(laughing)* Carried it where? Direct to video?

JERRY   *(to ALISON)* I didn't dress the salad. *(to RICHARD)* And we're off meat again!

RICHARD   That's okay I'm trying to cut down.

DIANE   Could I…. Another mineral water?

RICHARD   I'll get it.

JERRY   I'll help.

> *RICHARD and JERRY exit. A long pause.*

DIANE   You know Alison it's strange—when I first met you you were just a journalist to me and I never imagined that journalists have, you know, lives. I mean it's like teachers. When I was in school and I'd bump into a teacher, say at the grocery, I'd always be amazed that teachers you know ate or shopped or had families. It's as if they just disappeared when they weren't teaching, like they went into a frozen chamber or something. Like without me to teach they didn't exist. That's what journalists were always like to me.

> *Pause.*

But I guess it's different really—I mean in some ways without journalists I wouldn't exist.

> *Pause.*

I mean Diane Drake is a bit of an invention in a lot of ways. You know my real name isn't Drake. It's Briss. It's not even Diane. It's Bonnie.

Bonnie Briss. Which loosely translates into a *happy ritualistic circumcision*. It's the kind of name you kind of need to change if you're planning on seeing it in print. I like Diane Drake better. It's not like there's a Bonnie Briss anyway. Or I wonder. Some little, you know, entity wandering around wondering where I am…. Probably totally not.

ALISON   Probably totally not.

DIANE   Anyway. Are you all right?

ALISON   Probably totally not.

> *ALISON rises to pour herself some more wine. She stumbles slightly.*

DIANE   Maybe you should have some water.

ALISON   You're not drinking tonight Diane?

DIANE   I'm on a bit of a detox thing.

ALISON   A program.

DIANE   No! Just a… break. What a sweet little place you have.

ALISON   I'd give you the tour but Jerry just started ripping his office apart.

DIANE   Really? Why?

ALISON   A space thing. I thought we could move but he likes the house.

DIANE   Really. Yes it's cosy.

> *RICHARD and JERRY enter in the midst of a conversation. JERRY gives DIANE a glass of soda.*

JERRY   *(to RICHARD)* You've been saying that since you got out of university.

RICHARD   I am getting organized.

JERRY   You don't even wear a watch.

RICHARD   I don't like anything on my arms.

JERRY   Organized or not we are the image we project, projected back to us by the mirror of others. It's artificial.

RICHARD   All right all right.

JERRY   And all of these women—

RICHARD   *These women*, you make it sound like I'm some sort of Casanova.

DIANE   Which women?

ALISON   Richard's women.

RICHARD   All right Alison.

DIANE   What's he got, like a harem.

ALISON   Basically.

RICHARD   All right Alison.

ALISON   You're saying it's not like that?

RICHARD   No. Yes, no it isn't.

ALISON   Just in the past year! That girl from the bookstore, the girl from the phone thing—

RICHARD   Oh God…

DIANE   Do tell!

RICHARD   It wasn't a phone thing.

ALISON   It was the internet.

RICHARD   It was nothing.

ALISON   The lesbian.

RICHARD   She was bisexual.

ALISON   I liked her.

RICHARD   Alison…

ALISON   What was her name?

RICHARD   Peggy. We were just friends.

ALISON   (to DIANE) *Just friends* to Richard means he doesn't have his own toothbrush at your place.

RICHARD   I didn't know you were keeping a list.

ALISON   A partial list.

RICHARD   And your point exactly is?

JERRY   What we were talking about was projection.

DIANE   Oh projection. That can be dangerous. I've had projection several times. Actors get it all the time.

ALISON   You don't *get* projection you experience projection.

DIANE   You can get it—I've had it.

ALISON   You can't *have* it.

DIANE   I know what I've had and I've had it.

ALISON   It's not a venereal disease.

DIANE   I beg your pardon.

JERRY   Hey it's just language— simple vibrations in the diaphragm.

ALISON   *(to JERRY)* I thought language was all we had to go on.

JERRY   Nope—it's just a response to the idea of the self as an entity separate from the thing we call me.

ALISON   Right.

DIANE   So Jerry, I hear you're doing some renovating.

JERRY   Well not renovating really—

ALISON   I would call putting in a window renovating.

DIANE   Show me. I'm thinking about doing some work on my place.

JERRY   Sure but... are we ready to eat?

ALISON   Go ahead.

JERRY   Okay. Come on.

DIANE   Great.

> *JERRY and DIANE exit.*

RICHARD   Hey what's your problem cool down. You're so giving me a hard time in front of her. And you never liked Peggy at all.

> *RICHARD pours himself and ALISON more wine. ALISON steps forward and looks out into the audience as if waiting for something. RICHARD takes out a vial and snorts some powder off his hand as he speaks.*

Did I offend her? I think I offended her. Do you think she likes me? She intimidates me, she's so... translucent. You know? I'm all clammy. Are you clammy? I'm so clammy. You know this morning I couldn't decide between a shower and a bath. So I smoked a joint and I thought about it and I thought you know I prefer showers but maybe baths are better for me. You know soaking the body as opposed to just running water over it. But maybe I don't want to feel my body as intensely as I would in a bath—like I live my life so much outside my body that a shower is preferable—you know just a comma of awareness as opposed to a whole sentence of awareness. Which is maybe all about how much I hate myself. So I didn't take either—a shower or a bath. Do you think I offended her? Alison? I'm so clammy. Alison? What are you doing?

ALISON   Waiting.

RICHARD   For what?

ALISON   Waiting. Waiting.

DIANE enters followed by JERRY.

DIANE   I have to go.

RICHARD   Huh?

JERRY   Diane.

DIANE exits briefly and returns with her coat.

RICHARD   What's going on?

JERRY   Nothing.

DIANE   This was a mistake.

RICHARD   Are you okay?

DIANE   I have to go.

JERRY   Now. Look.

RICHARD   I'll give you a lift.

DIANE   No. Thank you.

JERRY   Stay.

DIANE   Do you want me to stay?

RICHARD   Of course.

DIANE   I'm asking Jerry. Do you want me to stay Jerry?

JERRY   Yes.

DIANE   All right I'll stay. I'll stay because I have something to say.

RICHARD   What?

DIANE   I'm pregnant.

RICHARD   Huh?

JERRY and DIANE exit. RICHARD leaves passing behind ALISON.

ALISON   *(to the audience)* Retrospect is everything…. It is the road ahead of you and the horizon behind you. In retrospect it all comes together. All the little details turn into that road map you didn't know you'd been following all this time. All this long time. And in retrospect we look back to see how we got there. What it must have been that got us there, how it must have happened.

DIANE appears on the other side of the stage. She drinks coffee from a styrofoam cup and holds a doughnut. Soon JERRY joins her. ALISON watches them.

JERRY   Hi there.

DIANE   Oh gosh hey, hi there.

JERRY   Jerry.

DIANE   No I know. I'm Diane.

JERRY   No hey I know. Hi.

DIANE   Hi. Listen I'm just so thrilled to meet you.

JERRY   Oh yeah?

DIANE   I thought I'd meet you in LA at the reading.

JERRY   Yeah no I have a… other job.

DIANE   No I know yeah, you're a psychiatrist.

JERRY   Yeah. A… well, a psychologist. I thought a PhD would be more challenging than Med School.

DIANE   Right. Well whatever you are you're a great writer. The script is brilliant. You really understand people—

JERRY   Really. Well.

DIANE   The situation's so real. The characters are so authentic.

JERRY   Yeah?

DIANE   I read so much crap. Jerry? I read so much crap? An actor is so grateful for this kind of writing.

JERRY   Well I've really loved your work that I've seen you do.

DIANE   I don't want to talk about me.

JERRY   Oh… I…

DIANE   No I'm sorry. I don't mean to be whatever, but really I want to talk about your script. I can't believe you haven't written before.

JERRY   I've written—you know stories and—

DIANE   You're born to write film. Really. And you got this together on your own!

JERRY   Yeah, no well, it was my wife really who pulled all this together, pulled in favours, you know, got it going.

DIANE   Your wife?

JERRY   Alison?

DIANE   Oh Alison right right Alison right. Oh you guys are married oh. She's sweet. I know Alison.

JERRY   Yeah.

DIANE   I was married once. For about ten minutes. I was a bit much for him I guess.

JERRY   Yeah. I mean you seem independent.

DIANE   Do I?

JERRY   Yeah.

DIANE   Looks are deceiving aren't they.

JERRY   I've heard that.

DIANE   Do you have any kids?

JERRY   Oh. No. I'm sorry. Uh.

DIANE   What?

JERRY   Just uh. My wife…. Alison last year she miscarried…. Or well it was almost full term so…

DIANE   Oh gosh I'm so sorry. It must be terrible.

JERRY   It's been really difficult for her. I can't… even myself really, even imagine what it must be like. For me it was still a kind of abstraction, the whole notion or the possibility of a child.

DIANE   Uh huh.

JERRY   But for her it was… well… real.

DIANE   Uh huh.

JERRY   But it's forced me to be more… fatalistic. Not in the sense of…. Not so much with the Calvinistic implications of the idea.

DIANE   Uh huh uh huh.

JERRY   Perhaps it's just simplistic rationalization; to buffer the pain.

DIANE   Uh huh. No, you know I was up for something once where that was the situation. That I would have had to play? And when I was preparing I went there? And it was just…. What a terrible terrible…. I'm sorry…. I'm such a sap…. I'm sorry.

JERRY   No. Yes. It's a very emotional thing.

DIANE   You can't even look at me sideways and I start to cry.

JERRY   It must be difficult.

DIANE   Well…. You know…

JERRY   But a wonderful gift as well. To be so responsive.

DIANE   Yeah. Well thanks. Yeah.

JERRY   I wish my patients could be so connected. But I guess if they were they wouldn't be my patients would they? Put me out of a job.

DIANE   You've got a new job now.

JERRY   Thank you.

DIANE   Can I give you a hug?

JERRY   Uh. Sure.

> *DIANE hugs JERRY.*

DIANE   Thanks.

JERRY   Yeah. No. Thanks.

DIANE   Anyway.

JERRY   Anyway.

DIANE   I am so late.

JERRY   Ah they're always behind.

DIANE   Exactly.

JERRY   Can I get you something?

DIANE   I should go.

> *DIANE gives JERRY her doughnut.*

But could you take this doughnut, it is so stale? I don't really mind myself it's just the crew, it's important to keep the morale up.

JERRY   I'm with you there.

> *DIANE exits. JERRY watches her go then exits.*

ALISON   And sometimes it's much worse then you imagined.

> *TOMAS appears. He wears a dressing gown and carries two glasses of champagne.*

TOMAS   What are you saying darling?

ALISON   Never mind.

> *TOMAS gives ALISON a glass of champagne. He watches her.*

What?

TOMAS   I could get used to this.

ALISON   To what?

TOMAS   Contentment.

ALISON   Oh you'd just get tired of contentment soon enough and be back to insignificance.

TOMAS   You are a fascinating woman.

ALISON   No I'm a woman who got hurt and instead of getting angry tried to get mellow—but not having the metabolism for mellow she just got cold.

TOMAS   You weren't so cold a few minutes ago.

ALISON   I know when to turn it on and off. I'm like a tap.

TOMAS   Let's go somewhere tonight.

ALISON   I'm working tonight.

TOMAS   What can a person possibly write about a party?

ALISON   People do it all the time.

TOMAS   And for what?

ALISON   Five dollars and fifty cents a word.

TOMAS   Yes well this is America.

ALISON   No. This is a hotel room. And as I remember King of the Gypsies it was my credit card we left at the desk?

TOMAS   Do you need money?

ALISON   Everybody needs money.

TOMAS   Don't go yet.

ALISON   What Tomas?

TOMAS   You shouldn't hate her so much.

ALISON   Hate who?

TOMAS   Diane. You know that scene you love from "Hector Finch"? With the couple, on the bridge, with the flower? It was Diane's idea—she improvised it—I had no idea until it happened. All of it, the tearing, the pocket, the river. It was all Diane. Just know she has some good in her. Don't hate her so much.

ALISON   It's not her I hate.

TOMAS   Come and live with me awhile in Mexico, let me take care of you.

ALISON   *(turning away)* I don't want to be taken care of Tomas. Look you're a nice guy, you come into town once in awhile, we get together. Let's not turn it into something it isn't.

TOMAS disappears.

(turning back to TOMAS) I'm sorry, I shouldn't have said that. Tomas? I'm sorry. Tomas?

PHILIP GARAY appears with a drink.

PHILIP   You're late. Here's the story up to ten minutes ago. Liana Faulkner is losing the plot, keep an eye on that. David Clarke brought his boyfriend but he's telling everyone he's somebody's cousin from Palm Springs—get in there. And Barry Brooks is predictably drunk. But just say *predictably present*. People will get it. I'm off to the "Craven Image" party. God knows why, those vodka people are doing it, cardboard canapes served by runway rejects.

ALISON   Philip I was thinking I could maybe get back into interviews.

PHILIP   Ah, a beggar and a chooser?

ALISON   It's not that I don't appreciate you getting me the work. I just think a feature would be nice.

PHILIP   You think I'd be doing this if I could swing a feature? Have you had something to eat? The Pad Thai's not terrible. Oh why so glum chum, come on. This is important work we're doing here. We're chronicling the social spin of an age. Think Warhol. Think…. Oh God I've been saying "Think Warhol" for fifteen years, does anybody even remember Warhol? Those were the days. Damn Mary Hart and the whole steaming heap of them. I don't know. It's not like it used to be. It's not like at *Charles*. I mean, can you believe I'm working for a magazine called *Fuck*? Oh well, nothing to do but toughen up.

ALISON   I'm just getting a little tired of this.

PHILIP   I've been tired since Apollo One. Listen darling, when in doubt just imagine you're giving people something to think about other than cancer and war. Or I don't know, just think of it as revenge, it works for me. I've got to run. Oh and give my apologies to Justin.

ALISON   Who's Justin?

PHILIP   Justin. You've met him. We've been together a couple of times.

ALISON   You're seeing someone?

PHILIP   Can we not get into it right now? Here he comes. Say anything.

PHILIP exits. JUSTIN enters.

JUSTIN   Hey! Phil! Philip! What's up? Hang on Phil I gotta get my coat. Shit. Faggot.

ALISON   Pardon me?

JUSTIN   You a friend of his?

ALISON   Yes I am.

JUSTIN   He owes me two hundred and fifty bucks.

ALISON   May I ask for what?

JUSTIN   My youthful company.

ALISON   I find that hard to believe.

JUSTIN   Why's that?

ALISON   You're not that young. What, is he paying by the week?

JUSTIN   *(laughs)* Can I buy you a drink?

ALISON   I don't think so.

JUSTIN   Ah baby come on.

ALISON   "Baby?"

JUSTIN   Come on no strings. No strings on me baby.

ALISON   That's what Pinocchio said and look what happened to him.

JUSTIN   What happened to him?

ALISON   He fell down didn't he.

JUSTIN   No, he got to be a real boy.

ALISON   Is that what you're looking for, a real boy?

JUSTIN   Why? Cause of Phil? Not likely. I only go with the lonely old guys cause they don't want much more than company.

ALISON   What do you think, I'm some lonely old lady in need of some company?

JUSTIN   No I think you're hot. What do you think of me?

ALISON   I think you're a cocky little bastard.

JUSTIN   Yes ma'am I am. Let me buy you a drink.

ALISON   No.

JUSTIN   No? Okay.

ALISON   I'll buy you a drink.

> *The light slowly shifts, they move closer together. Through the dialogue ALISON takes off her shoes and JUSTIN takes off her dress. She wears a light-coloured slip.*

JUSTIN   You got any enemies?

ALISON   Why?

JUSTIN   Cause I'll take care of whoever it is.

ALISON   You will will you?

JUSTIN   Or I can get somebody to. I got lots of friends.

ALISON   I bet you do.

JUSTIN   You know it.

ALISON   Connie Hoy.

JUSTIN   That's your enemy?

ALISON   Yes. With her perfect little house and her perfect little family.

JUSTIN   She got a dog? I know a guy who could take care of it.

ALISON   Can't we just give her cancer or something?

JUSTIN   We can do anything. We got the power to do anything to all the fuckers of the world. Nobody should be mean to you. You're special.

ALISON   Am I?

JUSTIN   You're beautiful.

ALISON   What's your name again?

JUSTIN   Justin.

JUSTIN takes a vial out of his pocket.

ALISON   Just in case. Just in time. This just in.

JUSTIN   You know it. Mmmmm you smell nice.

ALISON   You need a shower.

JUSTIN   You wanna get high?

JUSTIN offers her white powder from the back of his hand.
ALISON snorts the powder.

ALISON   And I want to stay high.

JUSTIN   That can be arranged.

ALISON   Good.

They begin to make love.
Light becomes a strobe. JUSTIN exits. ALISON stumbles back and forth across the stage eventually sinking to the floor, her head down. Light slowly fades up. JUSTIN reappears with a full glass of wine which he places on the floor beside ALISON.

JUSTIN   It's fucking Steven Spielberg. *(JERRY enters. ALISON remains seated on the floor.)*

JERRY   *(to JUSTIN)* Shouldn't you be somewhere? Like in jail?

JUSTIN   Shouldn't you fuck off?

JERRY   Charming.

JUSTIN   Fuck you fuck.

JERRY   Could you maybe say one sentence without *fuck* in it?

JUSTIN   I don't talk in fucking *sentences*. Faggot.

JERRY   Is he living here? Have you got this little prick living here?

JUSTIN   Hey! You want a fucking smack? Hey!

ALISON   Justin! Go! Go!

   JUSTIN exits.

JERRY   Jesus Alison.

ALISON   What?

JERRY   What is this?

ALISON   What is what?

JERRY   What are you doing?

ALISON   Thinking.

JERRY   Do you know what he does for a living?

ALISON   He's helping me with my schedule.

JERRY   He's a gigolo.

ALISON   *(getting up off the floor)* Oh for Christ's sake Jerry, update your thesaurus.

JERRY   I'm not paying his way.

ALISON   Whatever Jerry whatever.

JERRY   So what was so urgent you had to see me?

ALISON   Oh right. Oh right oh right. I just need a little loan. A little one.

JERRY   We still owe money on the movie.

ALISON   I thought it was number one in Japan or something.

JERRY   It's the number eight rental in Thailand and we still owe money on it.

ALISON   Okay but this is just short term.

JERRY   You don't look so good Alison.

ALISON   Exactly, which is why I need a little loan to get it together you know.

JERRY   How much?

ALISON   Ten thousand.

JERRY   What?!

ALISON   Five thousand.

JERRY   Christ Alison.

ALISON   Two thousand.

JERRY   Give me a couple of days.

>   *JERRY looks at ALISON, a moment.*

I think you need to slow down a bit.

ALISON   Exactly I know I do exactly.

JERRY   And listen Alison, I want to tell you this before you hear it from someone else. Diane and I are separating. It's mutual. It's the best thing. And she's going to take Rebecca—which is best. Diane will take the house, and Rebecca's starting school next year so, I think it's best this way.

>   *JERRY leaves. ALISON rises, stumbling and yelling after him.*

ALISON   Best. Best. Best. You son of a bitch.

>   *RICHARD enters carrying a sad little birthday cake lit with four candles. JUSTIN enters behind, dressed to go out. He carries a bottle of wine with which he refills ALISON's glass.*

RICHARD   *(singing to the tune of "Happy Birthday")*
I hate this song
I hate this song
I really love you
But I hate this song.

ALISON   Oh wow.

JUSTIN   What the fuck's that? What's wrong with the song?

>   *ALISON blows out the candles.*

RICHARD   Sorry.

JUSTIN   It's a good fucking song.

ALISON   I blew out all the candles.

JUSTIN It's not even her fucking birthday.

ALISON What?

JUSTIN Her birthday's tomorrow. It's only fucking ten o'clock.

ALISON Richard! It's not even my birthday yet! I blew out my candles and everything. Is that bad luck? Is that bad luck?

JUSTIN No shut up. You just might not get your wish that's all.

ALISON Oh no! I forgot to wish!

JUSTIN That's good then, you'll wish tomorrow when it's really your birthday. Fuck.

RICHARD Sorry I just thought... we were already celebrating you know. I made it myself.

ALISON Awww, thanks.

JUSTIN cuts himself a piece of cake and takes a bite.

RICHARD *(to ALISON)* Are you going to make any resolutions?

JUSTIN That's fucking New Year's.

RICHARD No but you can make a resolution anytime.

JUSTIN Yeah I made a resolution. No more of your fucking cake.

JUSTIN throws his piece back on the cake.

We gotta go soon Al.

RICHARD I was thinking about making a resolution.

ALISON Oh yeah.

JUSTIN We gotta go soon Al.

ALISON We gotta go soon Richard.

RICHARD Where?

ALISON *(to JUSTIN)* Where?

JUSTIN We got two parties baby. That movie thing and something at 1:30.

ALISON *(sitting on the floor)* One-thirty. That's so late.

JUSTIN It'll be fun.

RICHARD What is it? I'll come.

JUSTIN It's work.

RICHARD You're going.

JUSTIN   I'm her assistant.

RICHARD   Oh.

JUSTIN   We gotta go soon Al.

RICHARD   (*sitting on the floor beside ALISON*) I was thinking about making a resolution. Alison?

JUSTIN   Are you going to do something with your hair?

ALISON   Oh I know, I know.

JUSTIN   It's a fucking mess.

ALISON   I know. I need my hat.

JUSTIN   Which hat?

ALISON   Witch Hat? Fucking *Witch Hat* what?

JUSTIN   Which of your many fucking hats do you want?

> *JUSTIN exits to get ALISON a hat.*

ALISON   (*calling after JUSTIN*) The… the one… the other one…

RICHARD   Guess who died.

ALISON   Oh no. Who?

> *As he speaks RICHARD fumbles through a series of little plastic dope packages in his pocket, all of them empty.*

RICHARD   Connie Hoy. Cancer. She and Steeves were still together. Three kids. This is last year or something. She was sick for awhile I guess. I mean I saw her at the airport a couple of years ago and she seemed fine. She seemed happy.

ALISON   Nobody's happy.

RICHARD   No. But she seemed fine. It can just happen like that. The world can just end. But it does all the time. The world ended lots of times. The Permian Age. Ever hear of the Permian Age? 250 million years ago ninety-five percent of the world's species were wiped out. Happens all the time. Some little species is just walking along or swimming along and then just like that. Over. The Connie Hoy Age ended. The world ends every time. The Richard Age. The Alison Age. I was thinking about making a resolution. I was thinking of maybe cleaning up a bit. I'm feeling kind of sick all the time. Maybe we could clean up together.

ALISON   Clean up what?

RICHARD   I don't know. Nothing.

JUSTIN re-enters with a cardboard box. He drops it near ALISON.

JUSTIN   Here pick a fucking hat.

ALISON goes through the box pulling out hats, books, a walkman, speakers, gloves, more hats.

Richard buddy we gotta go.

RICHARD   *(rising)* Okay. Yeah okay.

JUSTIN   See you later.

RICHARD   Can I get a bag off you?

JUSTIN   No problem. Fifty bucks.

RICHARD   I haven't got any cash.

JUSTIN produces two small plastic bags from his pocket.

JUSTIN   Owe me. Here owe me for two.

RICHARD   Yeah great thanks.

RICHARD moves to leave.

I'll see you later. Happy Birthday Alison.

ALISON   Yeah Happy Birthday.

JUSTIN   See ya later. Thanks for the cake.

RICHARD   Yeah thanks.

RICHARD leaves.

JUSTIN   Did you find a fucking hat yet?

At the bottom of the box ALISON comes across her bottle of sand. She takes it out and hugs it to her.

ALISON   Look! Oh look!

JUSTIN   Oh Christ.

ALISON   Look.

JUSTIN   Yeah whatever we gotta go.

ALISON   Feel it! It's warm! It's still warm like the desert!

JUSTIN   No it's warm like the fucking radiator it was sitting on.

ALISON curls up on the floor with the bottle.

Look I'm going, I got some deliveries to make. Are you coming?

ALISON   We killed Connie Hoy.

JUSTIN   What?

ALISON   We killed her.

JUSTIN   Who?

ALISON   Connie Hoy.

JUSTIN   Who the fuck's that?

ALISON   We killed her.

JUSTIN   Jesus I'm going. Get a fucking grip lady.

> *JUSTIN leaves.*

ALISON   It's still warm.... Happy Birthday to me... Happy birthday to me... I'm sorry... I'm sorry.

> *The light slowly shifts, growing dim. ALISON lies on the floor, mumbling to herself. We begin to hear the following recorded text. Slowly JERRY, DIANE and TOMAS enter in mourning clothes, they clear the stage. DIANE helps ALISON to her feet and helps her back into her dress and shoes.*

RECORDED VOICE   You have reached an automated messaging service:

ALISON & JUSTIN'S RECORDED VOICES   Everybody!

RECORDED VOICE   Can not take your call at this time. Please leave a brief message at the sound of the tone and your message will be promptly returned.

RICHARD'S RECORDED VOICE   *(drunkenly)* Alison? I was thinking. I was thinking about all the reasons of life. Of my life and everybody's life. All the reasons. And the ones I thought of, they weren't really reasons, and then the ones I did think of were all reasons of power and bullshit reasons—like my father, exactly like my father. He was right. Fuck. I never did anything. *(pause)* You know how I don't like stuff on my arms? I was thinking it was because of me—because of maybe me in another life in some kind of prison with handcuffs or ropes or something. I wonder where I'll go now. They say that about necks. If you've been hung. In my next life maybe I'll never wear a tie. I never fucking wore a tie in this one. I'm sorry Alison. I'm sorry. I love you. Bye.

> *JERRY, TOMAS and DIANE have left the stage. ALISON is now standing, facing the audience. From her pocket she takes out the folded paper we saw earlier. She opens it and begins to read it to us.*

ALISON   *(reading)* "If you try you can feel the wall—of this bubble, this shell we breathe around ourselves, this tiny room we live in all our lives. This tiny room filled with mirrors and barely room to move. And then one day something happens—something happens and you see where you are and you leave the room and you go out into the world and you realize we've all been so alone, locked in our bubbles, our shells, our tiny rooms, all so alone, all this time."

ALISON folds up the paper and puts it away.

It needs an ending but I can't seem to find one.

ALISON turns and faces upstage where a WAITER is setting up a table and two chairs for lunch. DIANE appears and the WAITER seats her. They speak quietly. Sound: a busy restaurant.

WAITER   May I bring you something to drink while you're waiting for your friend?

DIANE   Yes, a glass of red wine. And you can bring me a small market salad. I'll order an entree when—

WAITER   When your friend arrives.

DIANE   Yes. I'll keep the menu.

WAITER   Would you like some bread?

DIANE   No that's fine just the salad.

ALISON enters the restaurant area.

ALISON   Hi.

DIANE   Oh hi.

ALISON   Am I late?

DIANE   Don't worry about it.

ALISON   I'm still you know, *mañana, mañana.*

DIANE   I just got here myself. Sorry but I went ahead and ordered a salad. I didn't eat any breakfast.

ALISON   That's fine.

DIANE   You look good. You look rested.

ALISON   That's Mexico.

DIANE   It really stays with you doesn't it. I spoke to Tomas last night.

ALISON   Oh yeah.

DIANE   He said to say hi.

ALISON   Hi back.

DIANE   You look good, you really do.

ALISON   So do you.

DIANE   Oh I'm an old hag. Today. You should have seen me yesterday! I was that close to twenty-something. But you know what they say.

ALISON   Close only counts in horseshoes and hand-grenades.

DIANE   And elevators.

> *A beat. The WAITER arrives with DIANE's wine and water for ALISON.*

WAITER   Here you go.

DIANE   Oh great thanks. *(to ALISON; re: wine)* You don't mind.

ALISON   Oh no no. *(to WAITER; re: water)* Thank you.

WAITER   Can I get you a drink?

ALISON   Water's fine. And I'm just going to have a salad.

DIANE   Just a salad?

ALISON   I'm not that hungry.

DIANE   Do you want some bread? I can't I'm off wheat.

ALISON   No thanks—my appetite is... I've had this headache since yesterday.

DIANE   Oh.

ALISON   It's nothing it's nothing.

DIANE   You sure?

ALISON   Yes yes. *(to the WAITER)* Just a salad.

DIANE   And I'll have the poached salmon.

WAITRESS   *(taking the menus)* All right. Thank you.

> *The WAITER exits.*

DIANE   Did you hear Jerry got married again.

ALISON   Yeah, last year.

DIANE   No again again.

ALISON   You're kidding.

DIANE   Practice makes perfect.

ALISON   Honestly.

DIANE   Thanks for seeing me. Um.

ALISON   No that's—

DIANE   I just wanted to um. Tomas mentioned he told you we're planning on getting married.

ALISON   Yes. That's great.

DIANE   Well you know, what the hell. I can not work in Mexico just as easily as I can not work here. But I just wanted to, you know, thank you, for being a presence in Rebecca's life. It's been good. She likes you.

ALISON   Oh well that's…. Thanks.

DIANE   As strange as it's all been.

ALISON   As strange as it's all been. Look I'm just going to make a quick call—trying to change an audition time for tomorrow

DIANE   An audition?

ALISON   Oh it's nothing really—one way to Mexico and a new frock basically.

> *DIANE rises. She stops.*

DIANE   It looks like there's going to be a Christmas after all.

> *DIANE laughs. ALISON takes the flower from the vase on the table and hands it to DIANE. DIANE takes in and looks at ALISON. After a moment DIANE smiles and rips the flower in two, she gives one half to ALISON. ALISON takes the flower and then smiling throws it at DIANE. DIANE throws her half at ALISON. They are both laughing. DIANE exits. ALISON is alone a moment. The sound in the restaurant gets louder, her headache grows more severe. The WAITER returns with water. We can barely hear him over the din. ALISON's head is pounding. She rises from the table. Sound continues to build.*

WAITER   Are you all right? Ma'am? Are you all right?

> *The sound becomes prolonged. ALISON stands and steps briefly off stage. Immediately she falls back into the arms of the WAITER who lies her down on the floor. (This is a second actress, dressed as ALISON.) As the sound continues to build (the first) ALISON magically appears downstage with her bottle of sand. The sound continues to build. She pulls the cork out of the bottle and slowly pours it onto the floor. When the bottle is empty a woman appears. The sound suddenly stops. The woman is CONNIE HOY. The light returns to normal.*

ALISON   Hello?

CONNIE   Hi Alison.

ALISON   Oh my God.

CONNIE   Hi, it's Connie Hoy.

ALISON   I know, oh my God.

CONNIE   Welcome. *(to the audience)* Hi. We're just going to be another few minutes. *(to ALISON)* Everything's okay?

ALISON   I don't know.

CONNIE   Everything's okay.

ALISON   I've been so awful to you.

CONNIE   Hm?

ALISON   I've been so awful to you.

CONNIE   Yes you've carried me with you all this time. But that had nothing to do with me, that was all about you. Anyway you'll have lots of time to deal with that later. Alison? Where are you?

ALISON   Where am I?

CONNIE   Yes.

ALISON   I don't know.

CONNIE   You can be anywhere you like. Where would you like to be? A forest? A desert? A place with a river or a lake?

ALISON   A.... A place with a lake.

CONNIE   Okay. Good. So be there.

ALISON   Be there?

CONNIE   Don't think about it too much. Close your eyes and just be there. Are you there?

ALISON   Okay.

CONNIE   All right. Okay. How old are you?

ALISON   I don't know…

CONNIE   You can be as old as you want to be.

ALISON   Okay. Eighty… two.

CONNIE   Fine. What time of day is it?

ALISON   Dusk. Just before dusk.

CONNIE   Summer or?

ALISON   October.

CONNIE   Are you alone?

ALISON   Yes. No. I'm with someone.

CONNIE HOY disappears. RICHARD appears.

Someone I love.

RICHARD   It's chilly.

ALISON turns to look at RICHARD.

It's chilly.

ALISON   Yes.

RICHARD   The leaves are turning late again.

ALISON   Yes.

RICHARD   I've been thinking.

ALISON   Yes?

RICHARD   You know what I'm going to do one of these days?

ALISON   What?

RICHARD   I'm going to get myself some long sleeved t-shirts.

ALISON   What do you mean?

RICHARD   Some of those long sleeved t-shirts, I'm going to get some for myself.

ALISON   But you don't like anything on your arms.

RICHARD   I know.

ALISON   You won't even wear a watch.

RICHARD   I know. But my arms get cold you know.

ALISON   Are you cold?

RICHARD   I do. My arms do get cold.

ALISON   Maybe that's not a bad idea then. Some long sleeved t-shirts.

RICHARD   That's what I was thinking.

ALISON   Are you cold now?

RICHARD   No it's pleasant.

ALISON   Yes.

RICHARD   It's nice isn't it.

ALISON   Yes. It is.

RICHARD   You don't want to go inside do you?

ALISON   No I'm fine here.

ALISON looks out at the audience and smiles.

It's nice.

Fade to black.

In On It

l to r: Daniel MacIvor, Darren O'Donnell
photo by Dona Ann McAdams

Notes on the play

In On It has three distinct realities (which can and do overlap and fishtail); they are: The PLAY, The SHOW and The PAST. The PLAY is the story of Ray—more often than not there is a sense of this happening in a highly theatrical, artificial environment; The SHOW: which is happening now, here, tonight and mainly consists of and THIS ONE and THAT ONE discussing The PLAY and its development and then eventually their relationship and its development; and The PAST which consists of THIS ONE and THAT ONE meeting and becoming lovers.

Design

We travelled to many theatres during the development and touring of *In On It*, our design concept was to strip each of these theatres to the bare walls and use only two chairs. These chairs would look as if they could have easily been found somewhere in the building in which the play was taking place.

The states of The SHOW, The PLAY and The PAST were each indicated by a different lighting state.

The only blackouts were as indicated in the script.

The only props used were the two chairs, a grey sports jacket, a tissue and a set of keys.

The jacket and the two chairs are carefully tracked in the script based on many months of development and performance.

Style

In order to clearly delineate between the three realities in *In On It* we developed three different kinds of "styles" (in the most superficial sense) of acting. In the PLAY we would both perform out—to the audience—but react as if we were actually facing one another. (The script is written with this as an assumed style so that a stage direction like *BRENDA turns to RAY* indicates that the actor playing Brenda turns away from the audience and faces the other actor). In the SHOW we would maintain an awareness of the audience, stage directions indicate when we addressed the audience. In the PAST we would suddenly be inside a fourth-wall reality with no awareness of the audience whatsoever.

Story

The back-story we had for *In On It* was as follows: Brad is killed in a head-on collision with a blue Mercedes driven by a man named Raymond King. There is some question as to how this accident happened, there seemed to be no reason for the car to veer into Brad's lane. In order to give some reason for this "accident" (and to assuage his guilt for insisting that Brad drive his car that day) Brian creates the play about Ray, his suicide and the reasons for it. Brad in effect is returning "from the dead" to assist in the creation of the play (and show) on this evening. This story was valuable for the actors but it was not necessary that the audience "get" this story—the audience will get the story they need to get.

Finally

In the script the characters are called BRAD and BRIAN although they never refer to one another by name. This is so that the actors understand they are playing real characters and not some stylized version of such. It is very important that in any program listing for any future production of this play that the characters be listed as THIS ONE and THAT ONE—this is how each refers to the other—in this way the audience slowly comes to realize that these characters are not post-modern simulations. This helps to keep the audience guessing as to the nature of the play and causes them to continually re-evaluate their perception of such.

Special Thanks

To Darren O'Donnell, Kimberly Purtell and Richard Feren who were instrumental in developing this play through workshops and rehearsals.

In On It was developed and produced by da da kamera and had its world premiere at the Vancouver East Cultural Centre, in 2001, with the following company:

THIS ONE . . . . Daniel MacIvor
THAT ONE . . . . Darren O'Donnell

Directed by Daniel MacIvor
Lighting Design: Kimberly Purtell
Set Design by Julie Fox
Sound and Music Design by Richard Feren
Produced by Sherrie Johnson

Later on tour the role of THAT ONE was played by Jim Allodi.

•

In On It was developed with the assistance of the Traverse Theatre in Edinburgh, Scotland, the Philadelphia Fringe Festival, Festival Antigonish Nova Scotia, the High Performance Rodeo in Calgary, Alberta and the Studio Theatre in Washington DC.

Special thanks to Mark Russell and Lesley Gore.

Characters

THIS ONE (Brad, Ray, Miles, Lloyd, Pam, Irving)
THAT ONE (Brian, Doctor, Ray, Brenda, Terry, Lloyd)

In On It

Pre-show: A bare space brightly lit. Two simple black chairs sit side-by-side upstage left. A jacket lies centre stage as if having been casually dropped there. As pre-show music we hear a collection of Lesley Gore songs. The final song of the pre-show is "Sunshine Lollipops and Rainbows." With the final beat of this song the house and stage is plunged into darkness leaving only the jacket lit by a tight special. We sit in silence with this image for several seconds until we hear Maria Callas singing an aria from the mad scene of Anna Bolena by Donazetti. In the darkness we see the form of a man in a white (or light-coloured) shirt and a tie. He slowly enters from offstage. This is BRIAN. BRIAN approaches the jacket. He stands looking down at it. Slowly he picks up the jacket puts it on. As he adjusts the jacket we hear the beginning of screeching tires. The aria is brutally interrupted by a shriek. Light snaps to a special on BRIAN as he looks up at the audience. He addresses the audience.

BRIAN   There are the things that happen out of careful planning: two people have a wedding, someone builds a boat, a person writes a play. The things that happen around guest lists and blueprints and re-writes. And then there are the things that happen over which we have no control. The things that sneak up on us. The things that just happen. The arbitrary optional life-changing things that seem to make no sense the things we have to invent sense for. Lots of things. Little things: the music our lover listens to; bigger things: the way our health can come out from under us like a carpet on a hardwood floor; huge things: the blue Mercedes. I can only imagine it but when I do, it's like this: You're on the road doing some errands; you've got to exchange some tickets, pick up a prescription for somebody's migraine, the usual. You pull out onto the highway to save some time, in your big powerful fast machine, being come at by a lot of other big powerful fast machines, driven by people about whose level of mental health or blood alcohol you know nothing. That's a sobering thought, you go for the radio. Crap. Crap. More crap. Crap. Something familiar. Crap. Back to something familiar. Can't find it. Where was it? One-oh-one point what? Or? Before the sports after the metal. There it is! And in that tiny moment of taking your attention ever so briefly away from the big machine in your hands, the other guy veers into your lane and you look up just in time to see the headlights of the blue Mercedes.

BRAD speaks from the darkness.
The light slowly shifts from BRIAN's special into the SHOW state.

BRAD   Do you think that's a good way to start?

> *BRAD enters from the darkness and stands just on the edge of the light.*

BRAD   Do you think that's a good way to start?

BRIAN   Start what?

> *BRAD enters the light.*

BRAD   The show.

BRIAN   It's not a show it's a play.

> *BRIAN steps upstage and picks up one of the chairs. He carries it downstage.*

BRAD   Oh.
(to the audience) Hi.
(to an individual) Hey!

BRIAN   Are you here to help or?

BRAD   Oh. Sure. Sorry.

> *BRIAN places the chair downstage centre facing the audience.*

BRIAN   Now we can start.

BRAD   Haven't we started?

> *BRIAN takes off the jacket and offers it to BRAD. BRAD takes the jacket and puts it on.*

BRIAN   Now we're starting.

> *BRIAN steps away and takes up a position upstage right facing the audience. BRAD sits in the chair.*
>
> *Light snaps to PLAY state (two specials). BRIAN is the DOCTOR. BRAD is RAY.*
> *Sound of a muted heartbeat which continues throughout.*

DOCTOR   Good morning Ray.

RAY   Good morning Doc.

DOCTOR   How was your weekend?

RAY   Fine. You know, considering.

DOCTOR   Considering?

RAY   I haven't been sleeping.

DOCTOR   Really?

RAY   Just nerves and… dreams. Lots of dreams. I keep having this dream about a concrete boat. I'm on this boat—big type, you know, big like a ship practically. And it's floating on like a kind of a canal and it's made of concrete. Concrete blocks, concrete slabs. I keep thinking it should sink—but it doesn't. It's vaguely unnerving. What do you make of that?

DOCTOR   Well...

RAY   Dreaming about concrete boats.

DOCTOR   Not my beat really.

RAY   What's that?

DOCTOR   Not my major.

RAY   Right.

DOCTOR   But there are books, you know, dream, you know, dictionaries...

RAY   Right.

DOCTOR   Do you have a boat?

RAY   No.

DOCTOR   Maybe it means you should get a boat.

RAY   Should I?

DOCTOR   How's Brenda?

RAY   Good. She's thinking about going back to school.

DOCTOR   Oh yeah?

RAY   She never got her degree. Really just something to do. She also started going back to church. Which is I guess something that happens at a certain age. Or... I guess.

DOCTOR   And is Miles still in school?

RAY   No he's out, he's working.

DOCTOR   In?

RAY   Advertising.

DOCTOR   Advertising? Really? A professional.

RAY   I know. It seems like just last year I was teaching him how to ride a bicycle and now he's beating me at squash.

DOCTOR   That's the way. And your dad is settled in all right at the home?

RAY   Oh yeah. And the car's running fine and the weed killer's working.

DOCTOR   Ha ha ha.

RAY   How am I?

DOCTOR   Can I get you something?

Sound: the heartbeat accelerates.

RAY   Sorry?

DOCTOR   Can Eileen get you something?

RAY   What do you mean?

DOCTOR   A glass of water or…?

RAY   Oh. No. Thank you. No.

DOCTOR   Raymond.

RAY   What?

DOCTOR   I've been looking over your test results. There's nothing conclusive—we're going to need some more tests before we can say what's really going on.

RAY   What might be going on?

DOCTOR   We're looking at a number of possibilities.

RAY   Ranging from?

DOCTOR   I'm concerned.

RAY   You're concerned.

DOCTOR   I'd like to get you into the hospital for a couple of days.

RAY   The hospital?

DOCTOR   The tests are quite extensive.

RAY   When?

DOCTOR   This week if we can manage it.

RAY   Right away?

DOCTOR   That would be best yes.

RAY   Oh. Oh. Oh. What are you telling me?

DOCTOR   We're looking a number of possibilities.

RAY   Worst-case scenario?

DOCTOR   I can't—

RAY   Am I sick?

DOCTOR   Ray. It's like this—you've got to stay strong and you've got to stay positive. That's your job.

RAY   Oh my God.

DOCTOR   As for the sleeping I can give you something if you like.

RAY   Oh my God.

DOCTOR   Can I get you a glass of water?

RAY   Oh my God.

DOCTOR   We don't know anything yet.

RAY   Who's "we?"

DOCTOR   Sorry?

RAY   "We don't know anything yet." Who's "we?"

DOCTOR   Uh…. You and I.

RAY   Bullshit. Of course I don't know anything. I'm not supposed to know anything, that's how this works. I'm not part of your "we." Who's "we?" You and who? You and the entire medical profession? You and all the healthy people? You and Eileen? She's stupid you know. Did you know she was stupid? You have a stupid receptionist. She can't remember my name. I've been coming here longer than she's been working here and she can't remember my name. That's just stupidity. Or malice. But she doesn't appear bright enough to be malicious.

DOCTOR   Raymond you're upset it's perfectly understandable.

RAY   You're enjoying this aren't you?

DOCTOR   Pardon me?

RAY   You are. You love this. You get to play "Doctor." That's what this is all about isn't it?

DOCTOR   (*slight nervous laughter*) Ray. Let's just take a step back from this for a second shall we.

RAY   Look at you, you are loving this, you're laughing.

DOCTOR   I'm not—Ray you're upset it's normal.

RAY   Oh shut up. Who do you think you are? George Fucking Clooney?

DOCTOR   Okay Raymond.

RAY   And what's the white coat supposed to signify? How ridiculous. What, did you just come in from the lab? Who's the white coat for? The pert little stupid bitch receptionist out front?

Sound: the heartbeat is at its most rapid.
Note: BRIAN's white—or light-coloured shirt represents the lab coat.

DOCTOR   Mister King.

RAY   You're pathetic. I bet you wear it outside. I bet you plan little excursions to the coffee shop just so you can wear it in the street. Watching yourself in the windows. Aren't you something. God, I pity you. You're a fool.

Silence.
Sound: the heartbeat returns to normal.

DOCTOR   Can I get you a glass of water?

RAY   Yes please.

BRIAN steps away from the DOCTOR's spot.
Sound out and light snaps to SHOW state. BRIAN heads for the chair upstage left.

BRAD   How was that?

BRIAN stops in his tracks.

BRIAN   What?

BRAD   How was that?

BRIAN   How was that how?

BRAD   How was I as Ray?

BRIAN regards the audience briefly.

BRIAN   I don't think this is really the time to be talking about it.

BRIAN moves upstage and retrieves the second chair. He places it upstage right facing the audience.

BRAD   I'm just asking. Was the task fulfilled?

BRIAN   The task?

BRAD   Yeah.

BRIAN   Yes whatever.

BRAD   Okay then, I'll just keep doing what I'm doing.

BRIAN   Um.

BRAD   Yes?

BRIAN   It's just that it's not that Ray's angry.

BRAD rises, BRIAN takes the chair BRAD has been sitting in and places it upstage stage left facing the audience.

BRAD   He's not angry?

BRIAN   No.

BRAD   He's raving.

BRIAN   He's not raving.

BRAD   "George Fucking Clooney."

BRIAN   So?

> *BRIAN sits in the stage left chair he has just placed.*

BRAD   "Pert little stupid bitch?"

BRIAN   No I know but—

BRAD   How else then?

> *BRAD takes off his jacket and offers it to BRIAN.*

How else?

> *BRIAN considers the audience a moment, he then takes the jacket from BRAD and puts it on as he crosses to the stage right chair. BRAD takes up a position ready to sit in the stage left chair. BRIAN takes up a position ready to sit in the stage left chair. (It is during this putting on of the jacket that BRIAN—unseen by the audience—takes a tissue from the pocket of the jacket and palms it in his left hand.)*

BRIAN   Like this.

> *Light snaps to PLAY state—one special only on BRAD.*
> *Sound: a busy restaurant at lunchtime.*
> *BRAD speaks as he sits. He is now MILES.*

MILES   Dad? Sorry I'm late. Damn rain. Dad? Ray?

> *Light snaps to PLAY state special on BRIAN.*
> *BRIAN speaks as he sits. He is now RAY.*

RAY   Oh. Miles. Yes. Hi. Sorry.

MILES   Sorry I'm late.

RAY   Not a problem.

MILES   Damn rain.

RAY   Yeah.

MILES   It was supposed to be sunny.

RAY   Was it?

MILES   Damn weathermen don't know a damn thing. They probably pick the damn forecast out of a damn hat. So I don't bring an umbrella this morning and now I've got to buy another—and we've got half a dozen at home.

RAY Well you know.

MILES Have you ordered? Dad?

RAY What?

MILES Have you ordered?

RAY Oh. No.

MILES The tortellini's terrible, the eggplant's soggy, the catch of the day is frozen and the specials aren't.

RAY Miles?

MILES Yeah?

RAY How's work?

MILES A farce. You know what Blanchard says to me this morning? "We've got to make plastic fun again." What? Hello? "Fun?" The old coot's got us some major plastics manufacturer as a client—no other agency in the western hemisphere would touch them no doubt. The world is ten minutes away from toxic implosion, skateboarders are running multinationals, the right is about to embrace hemp as the new miracle fiber and he wants to make plastic "fun" again. Anyways people aren't interested in fun anymore, people are interested in function. Oh, the veal's not awful.

RAY I saw the Doctor yesterday, I have to go for some tests.

MILES Yeah? I've got a mole I should get looked at. Does that look normal to you? Actually it looks fine here—it's probably just the ridiculous bulbs in the damn bathroom. Julie insists on the lowest wattage she can find—what is that, twenty or something? In terms of aging she's of the opinion that if you can't see it it ain't happening. Oh yeah hey we've got tickets for the opera at the conservatory next week and we can't use them. I know Mom was talking about it. Do you think you guys would be into it? I'd love to but Julie's got her French club. I don't know why she doesn't write this stuff down. Well I mean she does but…. Okay what is this? She pretends to make lists. Okay I mean she makes the lists but she never looks at them again—I mean she never consults them again—never scratches anything off them. What is that? That is not a list. That is just a piece of paper with words on it. A list needs to be updated, altered, checked. That's what makes it a list. And she keeps losing them. I know because I keep finding them. I mean I'm sorry but there are the kind of people who make lists and the kind of people who lose things—these are mutually exclusive qualities. I mean

"Let's face the facts Julie!" You know? "Let's live in the damn world Julie."

    RAY drops his head and begins to weep.

Dad? What's going on? Dad? Stop it. For God's sake. Dad you're making a scene.

RAY   I'm sick.

MILES   What?

RAY   I'm sick.

MILES   No you're not, stop it.

RAY   I have to go into the hospital.

MILES   For what?

RAY   For tests.

MILES   Tests. Tests are just tests. People go for tests all the time.

RAY   I'm sick.

MILES   How sick?

RAY   They don't know.

MILES   Yeah well tests see. Tests. Then they find the thing then they test the thing then they fix the thing. Dad? Right? Come on. Here.

    MILES raises his empty left hand toward the audience. RAY raises his left hand toward the audience and reveals the tissue he has been palming — the effect being that MILES has handed RAY a tissue.

You're all mucousy.

    Silence.

How come Mom didn't call me?

RAY   I didn't tell your mother yet.

MILES   Well who'd you tell?

RAY   Nobody. Just you.

MILES   You told me first? Why'd you tell me first? Don't be telling me stuff like this first. I'm no good with stuff like this. Don't tell me this stuff first okay.

RAY   Sorry.

MILES   That's okay but just you know.

RAY   Sorry.

MILES   Tell Mom. Don't tell Mom you told me. Just tell Mom. Tell Mom you told her first. She'd want you to, you know, tell her first. Tell her first and then she'll call me and I'll talk to Mom and then everything will be okay. Okay? Okay Dad?

RAY   Okay.

MILES   Should we have a drink? Do you want a drink?

RAY   Sure.

MILES   I'm a little hungry. How are you? Are you hungry?

RAY   I could eat.

MILES   I'm pretty hungry.

RAY   How's the veal?

MILES   Excellent.

> *MILES looks out the window.*

Damn!

RAY   What?

MILES   It stopped raining! And I already bought a damn umbrella.

> *Sound: fades out.*
> *An uncomfortable pause. BRIAN rises, light snaps to SHOW state.*

BRAD   *(to the audience)* It doesn't end very well.

BRIAN   *(to BRAD)* What?

BRAD   Nothing. And you got an opera thing in there.

BRIAN   Yes.

BRAD   So we'll be expecting a bit of opera? Beyond what we've already had?

BRIAN   Problem?

BRAD   No.

BRIAN   Good.

BRAD   So why is Julie such an idiot.

BRIAN   Julie?

BRAD   The wife.

BRIAN   Yeah I know—What about her?

BRAD   She's basically an idiot.

BRIAN   Not necessarily.

BRAD   We never meet her do we?

BRIAN   No.

BRAD   All we've got to go on is what Miles says about her?

BRIAN   So?

BRAD   So.

BRIAN   So.

BRAD   So basically she's an idiot.

BRIAN   I don't see that.

BRAD   So what does Julie represent?

BRIAN   Julie's not important, she's a secondary character.

BRAD   But she must represent something.

BRIAN   No.

BRAD   And what about Elaine?

BRIAN   Who?

BRAD   Elaine the secretary.

BRIAN   Eileen.

BRAD   Eileen yeah.

BRIAN   The receptionist.

BRAD   And she's what? Stupid?

BRIAN   What are you getting at?

BRAD   Not long on positive women.

BRIAN   Pardon me?

BRAD   Nothing, just some people might think you have a problem with women.

BRIAN   I don't have a problem with women.

BRAD   I'm not saying you do, I'm just saying—

BRIAN   If anyone has a problem with women you have a problem with women.

BRAD   I do?

BRIAN   Yes.

BRAD   In what way?

BRIAN   In lots of ways.

BRAD   For example?

BRIAN   For example…. When Kate brought… what's-her-name over to meet us…

BRAD   Emma?

BRIAN   No.

BRAD   Laura?

BRIAN   No the one with the tattoos and the bone in her nose.

BRAD   Gwen. It wasn't a bone.

BRIAN   Gwen. When Kate brought Gwen over to meet us *(to the audience)* we're having dinner and That One starts talking about… wetness.

BRAD   About what?

BRIAN   Wetness.

> *BRIAN picks up the chair he had been sitting in and places it upstage far stage right facing stage left.*

BRAD   *(to the audience)* Female ejaculation.

BRIAN   Yes and that sort of thing yes.

BRAD   I think it kind of turned her on actually.

BRIAN   Oh that's sweet.

BRAD   What's so potentially offending about it?

BRIAN   Oh come on.

BRAD   No really.

> *BRAD rises. BRIAN approaches BRAD, picks up the chair BRAD had been sitting in and then places it upstage far stage right close beside the chair he has just placed.*

BRIAN   You don't know where a person comes from, what their particular experiences are, how they're affected by things.

BRAD   It's just a conversation.

BRIAN   She may have been a Christian.

BRAD   Christians ejaculate.

BRIAN   She might have had issues.

BRAD   Like what?

BRIAN   Like whatever.

BRAD   You are so status quo.

BRIAN   What does that mean?

BRAD   You're dealing with things around this idea of men are like this and women are like this which quickly devolves into—

BRIAN   Oh please.

BRAD   That Asians are like this and Native Americans are like this.

BRIAN   Here we go.

BRAD   The point is if you're presenting women as bimbos and half-wits then you are just preserving the status quo which always presents women as bimbos and half-wits. I shouldn't have to tell you this.

BRIAN   You shouldn't have to tell me this?

BRAD   No just.... Sorry.

> *BRIAN takes off the jacket and presents it to BRAD.*

BRIAN   Brenda's not a half-wit.

> *BRAD takes the jacket and puts it on.*

BRAD   She's terrible to Ray.

> *BRAD and BRIAN take up positions downstage left and right facing out.*

BRIAN   Everybody's terrible to Ray, that's the point.

> *Light snap to PLAY state (two specials).*
> *Sound: distant opera on the radio.*
> *BRIAN is BRENDA, BRAD is RAY.*
> *Note: in becoming BRENDA, BRIAN crosses one arm over his chest and holds his other hand to his throat. By doing this BRIAN is doing two things: giving BRENDA a sense of feminine elegance and also hiding his tie.*

RAY   Brenda?

BRENDA   You're late.

RAY   I had a late lunch with Miles.

BRENDA   How's Miles?

RAY   Fine. He says he has some tickets for that thing at the conservatory—if you were interested—something you wanted to see?

BRENDA   Oh the Puccini.

RAY   I guess.

BRENDA   I read it was overstated.

RAY   Overstated?

BRENDA   Broad strokes. Lacking in subtlety.

RAY   Oh.

BRENDA   Apparently some Latin American director set it in a fish factory or a fruit farm or something.

RAY   Have you been drinking?

BRENDA   Oh shut up Ray.

RAY   Sorry.

> *Silence.*

Brenda? We need to talk.

BRENDA   Yes we do, I know we do, this is ridiculous, why do we bother, why do we even try, well we don't, that's just it isn't it, we don't try, we say we will, and with the best intentions, the best intentions, but we don't. I look at you Ray and I feel... *(long sigh)* ...love I guess. But it's static, it's dormant, there's nothing moving in here but... concern for you. And the longer I live like this the less I care. I'm calling it quits.

RAY   Brenda can I say something? I really need to say something.

BRENDA   I'm having an affair.

RAY   What?

BRENDA   With Terry Burke.

RAY   Who's Terry Burke?

BRENDA   Pam Ellis' husband.

RAY   Who's Pam Ellis?

BRENDA   Lloyd's mother.

RAY   Terry?

BRENDA   Yes.

RAY   The Christian?

BRENDA   There's nothing wrong with being a Christian, Ray.

RAY   Jesus Christ.

BRENDA   Exactly.

RAY   Who am I talking to?

BRENDA   He's a good man.

RAY   And a hypocrite. How long? How long?

BRENDA   Almost a year.

RAY   Oh that's sweet.

BRENDA   He told Pam yesterday—he's spending the day with Lloyd today.

RAY   What?

BRENDA   I'm sorry Ray but my life has opened up, I'm calling it quits. I've packed some things, I'll let you know where I am.

>   *BRENDA turns to RAY.*

What did you want to say?

>   *RAY turns to BRENDA.*

RAY   Is there such a thing as a concrete boat? Would a concrete boat float? It seems like it wouldn't. It seems like it would just sink.

>   *BRENDA turns away.*

BRENDA   I haven't the slightest idea.

>   *Silence.*
>   *BRIAN drops his arms to his sides.*
>   *Light snap to SHOW state. Sound out.*

BRIAN   See Brenda's not a half-wit.

BRAD   She's drunk.

BRIAN   She's not drunk she's been drinking.

BRAD   She's drunk.

BRIAN   She's upset. She's confused.

BRAD   What's next?

>   *BRAD and BRIAN exchange positions on the stage.*

BRIAN   *(to the audience)* A beautiful piece of music.

BRAD   Of course.

BRIAN   *(quietly to BRAD)* Problem?

BRAD   No.

BRIAN   Fine.

BRAD   Fine.

BRIAN   *(continuing to the audience)* Maria Callas—

>   *Sound: distant Maria Callas which transforms into a field: birds, a plane at one point flies distantly overhead.*

—singing the mad scene from Anna Bolena by Donazetti. Anna is on her way to her execution, she stops for a moment and in a sublime aria recounts the simple joys of her childhood.

BRIAN has taken a position upstage left.

BRAD   And then?

BRIAN   A field. Terry and Lloyd.

BRAD   Can I be Lloyd?

BRIAN   Sure.

BRAD wraps the jacket around his waist.
BRIAN throws an imaginary ball toward the audience.
Light shift to PLAY state.
BRAD becomes LLOYD. BRIAN becomes TERRY.
LLOYD jumps to catch the ball, misses. LLOYD chases the ball back and arrives in a special upstage left from where he plays the scene.

LLOYD   Sorry Terry.

LLOYD throws the ball back.
Note: the two play the scene out both throwing and catching toward the audience.
Sound: with each catch we hear the sound of the ball hitting a baseball glove, when LLOYD misses the ball we hear it hit the ground and roll along gravel.

You know there's like six billion people on the planet and four point six billion live in abject poverty.

TERRY   Whoa.

TERRY catches the ball, throws it back.

LLOYD   So like twenty percent of the population has eighty percent of the wealth and eighty percent of the population has like twenty percent of the wealth?

LLOYD catches the ball, throws it back.

TERRY   That's quite a bit huh?

TERRY catches the ball, throws it back.

LLOYD   And if you're talking about really really rich people…

LLOYD catches the ball, throws it back.

…there's only like maybe three hundred billionaires on the planet, so hardly any,

TERRY catches the ball, throws it back.

TERRY   Probably fit them all in this field.

> *LLOYD catches the ball, throws it back.*

LLOYD   Yeah and kill them all!

> *TERRY catches the ball.*

TERRY   Hey now…

LLOYD   Just kidding Terry.

> *TERRY throws the ball back. LLOYD catches it.*

But and plus, um, also there's enough food for everyone in the world—there don't need to be any starving people—

> *LLOYD throws the ball back.*

—it's just that letting food rot is more economically viable for the people who…

> *TERRY catches the ball.*

…the people who…

> *TERRY throws the ball back, LLOYD catches it.*

TERRY   Who makes the money off it.

LLOYD   Yeah.

> *LLOYD throws the ball back. TERRY catches it.*

Did you know that one North American produces more waste than twenty Chinese people.

> *TERRY throws the ball back. LLOYD misses it.*

Sorry Terry.

> *LLOYD runs out of light to get the ball. TERRY turns so that he is facing LLOYD.*

TERRY   You've got a good arm but you can't catch for shit.

> *LLOYD returns with the ball. He faces TERRY. Until indicated the two speak directly to one another.*

LLOYD   What?

TERRY   You've got a good arm.

> *LLOYD smiles. Silence.*

I'm going away.

LLOYD   What?

TERRY   I'm going away.

LLOYD   To Hamilton?

TERRY   No away away. Taking a break. Moving out.

LLOYD   Taking a break?

TERRY   Your mom and I need some space.

LLOYD   What do you mean?

TERRY   These things just happen Lloyd.

LLOYD   Right.

TERRY   But I just want to say it's been really great hanging out with you the last couple of years. I learned a lot of good stuff from you. And hey, it's not like I'm disappearing or anything. I'll be around. We'll stay in touch.

LLOYD   Do you think my dad might come back?

TERRY   I don't think so.

LLOYD   I didn't think so.

> *LLOYD turns to face out.*
> *TERRY turns to face out.*
> *They continue to throw the ball back and forth as before.*

TERRY   Hey! You know the apostles. Can you name them?

> *LLOYD throws the ball to TERRY.*

LLOYD   John.

TERRY   Good.

> *TERRY throws the ball to LLOYD.*

LLOYD   Peter. Andrew. Matthew.

> *LLOYD throws the ball to TERRY.*

TERRY   That's four.

> *TERRY throws the ball to LLOYD.*

LLOYD   Jacob and Simon.

TERRY   Six.

> *LLOYD throws the ball to TERRY.*

LLOYD   Phillip and Thomas.

TERRY   Eight.

> *TERRY throws the ball to LLOYD.*

LLOYD   Judas.

> *LLOYD throws the ball to TERRY, hard, TERRY almost misses it.*

TERRY   Three more.

> *TERRY throws the ball to LLOYD.*

LLOYD   Thaddeus. Bartholomew.

TERRY   One more.

> *LLOYD throws the ball to TERRY.*

LLOYD   The other Jacob.

> *TERRY catches the ball and holds on to it.*

TERRY   Jacob what?

LLOYD   Jacob Alphonse?

TERRY   No! Jacob Alpheus. But see, you learned some good stuff hanging out with me too.

> *TERRY throws the ball to LLOYD. LLOYD does not even try to catch it. The ball hits the ground.*
> *Silence.*

LLOYD   It's not like you were my real dad or anything anyway.

TERRY   No.

> *The two stand in silence for a moment.*
> *They step downstage, out of the light.*
> *After a moment: light snaps to SHOW state.*

BRAD   That's sad.

BRIAN   That's life.

> *BRIAN steps across the stage toward the chairs.*

BRAD   So Terry... he's only in the one scene?

> *BRIAN stops.*

BRIAN   Yeah.

BRAD   I see.

BRIAN   What?

BRAD   No no nothing.

BRIAN   It's not about Terry.

BRAD   I know but just... what purpose does Terry serve? I mean other than for you to explore your abandonment issues.

BRIAN   No no no no no. Terry represents an idea of God.

BRAD   Oh.

BRIAN   As Lloyd will come to later.

BRAD   Oh.

BRIAN   *(to the audience)* It's complex.

BRAD   Right. So nobody's happy?

BRIAN   Simplistically yes I guess.

BRAD   Nobody nobody.

BRIAN   Nobody nobody?

BRAD   Nobody everybody.

BRIAN   That would seem to be the case yes.

BRAD   Not you, not me.

BRIAN   We had our moments.

BRAD   But not happy?

BRIAN   No.

> *Sound: Lesley Gore's "Sunshine Lollipops and Rainbows."*
> *BRAD and BRIAN look at one another through the first verse of the song. BRIAN steps away toward the chairs up stage right. Light slowly shifts to a special on BRAD as the sound falls into the background.*
> *BRAD addresses the audience.*

BRAD   "How We Met." Our friend Kate was having a Commitment Ceremony with her girlfriend Jessica. This One knows Kate from forever. I know Kate from this lefty bookstore Kate and I used to work at. And as part of this Commitment Ceremony Kate wants all her friends—instead of bringing gifts—to do some kind of performance—because she's into that sort of thing. And she wants me to do a dance to this Lesley Gore song she loves—because she knows I love Lesley Gore. And I'm like "No Way!" but I can't say that so I just say "Yeah sure." Meanwhile This One's apparently supposed to be doing a lip sync to some Maria Callas song. But the thing is he's got this cabal... this coven of these twenty-five-year-old Trust-Fund-Opera-Buff types he hangs out with: The Assistant to the Dean of Antiquated Studies at the University of Fa Fa Fa and Little Miss Fox Fur and Little Miss Champagne and Sunglasses and Little Lord Lady's Day At The Track. These are the kind of people who think Counter Culture is a yogourt shop. Anyways. Story goes the Trust-Fund-Opera-Buffs put the kibosh on Maria Callas because apparently This One doesn't quite pass as a Maria Callas—or a Maria Anything I'd guess—and he was in danger of "embarrassing himself" which in the Trust-Fund-Opera-Buff world is second only to wearing brown shoes after six o'clock as something we "just can't have." So no Maria Callas—and This One has nothing to do at the Ceremony, so Kate suggests we get together on the Lesley Gore thing and I think, Great, this song is least Trust-Fund-Opera-Buff-type song you can imagine and I'll work up this ridiculous dance and he'll be like "Perhaps not" and I'll be off the hook.

> *BRAD leaps out of his light.*
> *Light snaps to The PAST.*
> *Sound: The last chorus of "Sunshine, Lollipops and Rainbows."*
> *BRAD finishes a ridiculous dance for BRIAN.*

BRIAN   Well.

BRAD   Yeah.

BRIAN   It's quite energetic.

BRAD   Yeah, you know. I do a lot of yoga.

BRIAN   Right. It's a bit…

BRAD   Um hm?

BRIAN   Athletic.

BRAD   Do you find?

BRIAN   I've got a kind of a bad back.

BRAD   Ooo that can be dangerous.

BRIAN   And it's Sunday?

BRAD   Yeah Sunday.

BRIAN   I work on Monday morning.

BRAD   Me too. And it can't be a late night.

BRIAN   No.

BRAD   And it's going to be a loooong evening.

BRIAN   How do you mean?

BRAD   A full program.

BRIAN   Oh right yes of course.

BRAD   How did you think I meant it?

BRIAN   In no way… just…. What do you think of Jessica?

BRAD   She's cool.

BRIAN   A little pushy though don't you find. For Kate?

BRAD   Pushy?

BRIAN   Opinionated.

BRAD   She has lots of opinions yeah—but so does Kate.

BRIAN   Oh that's a new thing.

BRAD   You don't like Jessica?

BRIAN   No just no you know.

BRAD   But she loves Kate.

BRIAN   Yeah she does love Kate.

      A beat.

BRAD   Are you still seeing?…

BRIAN   Gordon.

BRAD   Gordon?

BRIAN   No. Yes. No. Yes. No yes no yes. You know.

BRAD   Right.

BRIAN   On again off again.

BRAD   Right.

BRIAN   Basically it's a two-year relationship that's lasted for five years.

BRAD   *(laughing)* Been there buddy. So on now or off now?

BRIAN   Somewhere in between.

BRAD   Oh that hurts.

BRIAN   I like your jacket.

BRAD   Thanks.

BRIAN   It looks good on you.

BRAD   Thanks.

      A beat.

BRIAN   So Sunday…

BRAD   Yeah Sunday…

BRIAN   What the heck.

BRAD   What?

BRIAN   Well it is for Kate and everything right?

BRAD   What about your back?

BRIAN   Oh. I was bluffing about my back, my back's fine. Strong like horse.

BRAD   Oh.

BRIAN   So should we rehearse?

BRAD   What the heck.

> *BRAD takes off the jacket.*
> *Light slowly fades as:*

See sometimes we were happy.

BRIAN   No sometimes we weren't sad.

> *Light continues to fade slightly then suddenly snaps to PLAY state (two specials).*
> *BRAD becomes RAY.*
> *BRIAN becomes the DOCTOR.*

DOCTOR   Good Morning Ray.

RAY   Good Morning Doc. So what's the verdict?

DOCTOR   The verdict?

RAY   Let's cut straight to the chase shall we?

DOCTOR   I came across one of those dream dictionaries we were talking about I couldn't find concrete boat but it seems that boat represents a kind of rebirth.

RAY   What's the verdict?

DOCTOR   It's not good news.

> *BRIAN steps downstage as the specials cross fade. He covers his tie, one arm across his chest and one hand at his throat becoming BRENDA.*

BRENDA   But it's not the worst news, it could be worse.

RAY   Brenda?

BRENDA   Please Ray.

RAY   It's not good news—he said it's not good news.

BRENDA   But there are so many treatments—so many new treatments.

RAY   Brenda?

BRENDA   No.

RAY   No what?

BRENDA   I can't.

RAY   You can't what?

BRENDA   It's not healthy Ray. We're not healthy together. You're better off without me.

> *BRENDA lifts her empty hand.*
> *RAY lifts the jacket he holds as if BRENDA has just handed it to him.*

I brought you back your jacket. I took it with me when I left, I thought I might want something to remind me of you.

RAY   But you don't.

BRENDA   But I don't.

> *RAY throws the jacket on the floor at BRENDA's feet.*

RAY   Fuck you!

> *BRIAN drops his arms to his sides.*
> *Light snaps to SHOW state.*

BRAD   I don't buy it.

BRIAN   What?

BRAD   I don't buy it. So Brenda's just going to walk out on Ray?

BRIAN   Yes.

BRAD   Ray's dying and she doesn't care.

BRIAN   It's not about Brenda.

BRAD   It's all about Brenda right now.

> *BRIAN lifts his arms to the BRENDA position.*
> *Light snaps to PLAY state (one special).*
> *Sound: a distant opera.*

BRENDA   *(addressing the audience)* A word in my own defense in which I struggle with cliches to try and describe the sensation of something suddenly going out. Not like a candle—not like a short sharp breeze and a pop and a slow glow down to nothing and then smoke. This is more like a shutter slamming or a cover closing—but not like that because the shutter and the cover indicate something within. This is the kind of going out where something collapses into itself and without a flutter turns to air. It is the feeling of something suddenly going out which is forever strangely linked to the image of a lambswool jacket lying on the floor.

> *BRAD speaks from the darkness.*

BRAD   You're going to have to do better than that.

> *BRIAN drops his arms to his sides.*
> *Sound out.*
> *Light snaps to SHOW state.*

BRIAN   Better than what?

BRAD   I'm not convinced.

BRIAN   Of what?

BRAD   The depth of her feeling.

BRIAN   Excuse me?

BRAD   And you're stretching the metaphor.

BRIAN   The metaphor?

BRAD   With your Jacket Thing.

BRIAN   It's not My Jacket Thing.

BRAD   Okay. The Jacket Thing.

BRIAN   It's a different Jacket Thing.

BRAD   It's "The Jacket Thing."

> *BRIAN picks the jacket up from the floor and approaches BRAD.*

BRIAN   Brenda's leaving Ray because she can see what he's become.

BRAD   Which is what?

BRIAN   Which is just like everybody else.

BRAD   There is no "everybody else."

BRIAN   Oh that's deep.

BRAD   To you maybe.

> *Light snap to the past.*
> *Sound: distant Lesley Gore.*
> *BRIAN holds out the jacket to BRAD.*

BRIAN   Take the jacket.

BRAD   I don't want the jacket.

BRIAN   Then why did you bring it up?

BRAD   I just asked if you were going to be wearing it tonight.

BRIAN   Wasn't that apparent? Seeing I was wearing it at the time.

BRAD   Forget it.

BRIAN   Do you want to wear the jacket?

BRAD   No. I don't care.

BRIAN   Wear it if you want to.

BRAD   No. It is my jacket.

BRIAN   Then wear it.

BRAD   You have lots of jackets.

BRIAN   So.

BRAD   I have two.

BRIAN   You never wear this jacket.

BRAD   Because you're always wearing it. You've been wearing it ever since we moved in together. Since before. You took it from my closet.

BRIAN   It was at the bottom of your laundry bag, you never wore it.

BRAD   I used to wear it all the time before you claimed it.

BRIAN   Claimed it? Oh please take the jacket. What's your issue?

   BRIAN throws the jacket at BRAD. He catches it.

BRAD   I have no issue.

BRIAN   What's your issue?

BRAD   I don't like it when you wear my stuff.

BRIAN   What?

BRAD   It bugs me when you wear my stuff.

BRIAN   You're not serious.

BRAD   I know I know it's just a thing I don't know.

BRIAN   Okay okay I can accept that. It's petty but—and it certainly seems ironic coming from you.

BRAD   Ironic?

BRIAN   Ironic's a word.

BRAD   What's another word?

BRIAN   I thought we were supposed to end ownership.

BRAD   Nobody cares about the privatization of a jacket.

BRIAN   What's the difference?

BRAD   Maybe I have an emotional attachment to this jacket.

BRIAN   "Emotional attachment" oh that's an interesting argument from the man who claims to be above sentiment.

BRAD   I made no "claim"—

BRIAN   Watch out or you'll be joining me as just another cog in the "Patriarchal Industrial Bullshit Machine."

BRAD   I wasn't talking about you.

BRIAN   "Bullshit Machine." You accuse my friends of being poseurs. It's the same damn thing. It's all just a persona.

BRAD   What is your issue?

BRIAN   Mister "Noam Chomsky."

BRAD   *(laughing)* Is that all you've got?

BRIAN   Hypocrite.

> *BRAD throws the jacket on the floor at BRIAN's feet.*

BRAD   Fuck you!

> *Light snap to show.*
> *A beat.*

Try it again. Defend yourself now. Go on.

> *BRIAN steps down into BRENDA's spot. He faces the audience put his arms in the BRENDA position.*

BRENDA   I word in my own defense—

BRAD   What are you doing with your hands?

BRIAN   I'm hiding my tie.

BRAD   So she's wearing a tie.

> *BRIAN faces the audience.*
> *Light: slowly through the following cross fades from SHOW to PLAY (one special for BRIAN, BRAD in darkness.)*

BRIAN   A word in my own defense in which I struggle with cliches while searching for metaphors and come up with a grey lambswool jacket and something suddenly going out. A grey lambswool jacket lying on the floor and something suddenly… not like a candle, not like a short sharp breeze or a "pop" and a slow glow down to nothing and then smoke. This is sudden. And it leaves no trace. Just an un-nameable emptiness— a name would give it too much weight—caused by something suddenly going out—and leaving behind nothing. Nothing not even a nothing to hold up the nothing. And a grey lambswool jacket lying on the floor.

> *Light slowly fades to black.*
> *BRAD begins speaking in the darkness, as he speaks the light fades up to SHOW state. BRAD is sitting on the floor.*

BRAD   Is that how you felt about me? Empty? Not even a nothing to hold up a nothing? Is that why we were going to split up?

> *BRIAN picks up the jacket.*

BRIAN   Why did you get so upset about the jacket?

BRAD   Because the first time I wore it you said I looked good in it.

> *BRIAN approaches BRAD. He stands over him looking down. BRIAN offers the jacket to BRAD.*

You know there is such a thing as a concrete boat. People race them on a river in Missouri. I read about it in a magazine.

> *BRAD takes the jacket and puts it on.*

Lots of people go to watch.

BRIAN   Hey Mister King.

> *Light snaps to PLAY state. (One large special for LLOYD and RAY.) BRAD becomes RAY. BRIAN becomes LLOYD.*

RAY   Hey Lloyd.

LLOYD   Why are you sitting on our front lawn?

RAY   What?

LLOYD   You've been sitting on our front lawn for an hour.

RAY   I'm waiting for your dad.

LLOYD   He's not my dad.

RAY   Sorry. Terry.

LLOYD   He doesn't live here anymore.

RAY   Where is he?

LLOYD   I don't know. Hamilton maybe. Mrs. King's with him.

RAY   Are you telling me that Lloyd?

LLOYD   You knew?

RAY   I knew.

> *LLOYD sits beside RAY.*
> *RAY stares at the moon.*

The grass is wet.

RAY   Is it?

LLOYD   Do you know the Bible?

RAY Somewhat.

LLOYD Okay, so there's Adam and Eve and they have kids but who do their kids marry?

RAY I don't know.

LLOYD Seems weird. But you know the apostles right? How come when they wrote it they gave two of them the same name of Jacob. Why didn't they just give them different names so it wouldn't confuse people? Because somebody wrote it, right?

RAY I guess.

LLOYD Is it made up or is it true?

RAY It's whatever you want it to be I guess.

LLOYD Oh. Because the same-name thing kind of makes it seem like it is true. That that's how it really happened.

> *Silence.*
> *LLOYD looks up at the moon with RAY.*

You know it's like everybody lives in this big circle and everybody wants to be in the centre of the circle but the centre of the circle is the smallest part. There's no way.

RAY I'm dying.

LLOYD Everybody's dying.

> *RAY squeezes LLOYD's ear.*

BRIAN Ow!

BRAD Poor Lloyd.

BRIAN Poor Lloyd.

BRAD Who's Lloyd supposed to be?

BRIAN I think that's obvious isn't it?

BRAD What's going to happen to Lloyd?

BRIAN Oh he's going to grow up and become a computer geek and start an ingenious website and save the world and make a trillion dollars.

BRAD Do you think?

BRIAN I don't know. No. He just goes away when the play ends.

BRAD That's sad.

BRIAN That's life.

> *BRIAN gets up and walks out of the light. He takes up a position in the dark, parallel to BRAD but facing upstage.*
> *Sound: crowd at a wedding reception.*
> *Light cross fades to special for BRAD.*

BRAD   Cheers cheers cheers and best wishes to Kate and Jessica on their happy day. It looks like I'm the last act of the evening—but unfortunately my partner seems to have gone AWOL—but fear not, in true showbiz tradition—whatever that is—everything's coming up roses and the show must go on and all that. So. Hit it Kate.

> *We hear "Sunshine, Lollipops and Rainbows" in the background as BRAD addresses the audience.*

The day before we had been rehearsing at This One's place and Little Miss Fox Fur and Little Lord Lady's Day At The Track happened to be there and caught a bit of the act. Turns out they voted it "Silly" which in the trust-fund-opera-buff manifesto is a grade of the most horrific order and so This One acquits himself of the whole endeavor with not so much as a see-ya-later-sucker. A couple of nights later and I'm really pissed, in both senses of the word, and I dig up This One's phone number and decide to give him a piece of my irk.

> *Sound: a telephone rings.*
> *Light snaps up second special for BRIAN as he spins to face the audience.*

BRIAN   Hello?

BRAD   Hey.

BRIAN   Hey!

BRAD   Yeah so hey.

BRIAN   I was just thinking about you.

BRAD   You were?

BRIAN   Yeah. I had a great time the other night.

BRAD   You did?

BRIAN   I'm sorry I had to leave.

BRAD   Why did you leave?

BRIAN   I told you I had to work in the morning.

BRAD   Yeah I know but—

BRIAN   Come over.

BRAD   Come over?

BRIAN   Come over.

BRAD   Uh. It's a bit late.

BRIAN   I want to make love to you.

BRAD   Oh. Okay. Oh. Okay. I guess.

BRIAN   Hurry.

> *Light: BRIAN's special out.*
> *BRAD addresses the audience.*

BRAD   Now, normally I wouldn't do that kind of thing but it was… Wednesday.

> *Light quick black.*
> *Sound: a noisy doorbell.*
> *Light snaps up to past. BRAD and BRIAN face one another.*

Hey.

BRIAN   Oh hi.

> *Silence.*

BRAD   Aren't you going to invite me in?

BRIAN   I'm kind of expecting someone.

BRAD   Yeah, me.

BRIAN   No, Gordon's coming over.

BRAD   Why didn't you tell me that?

BRIAN   Tell you that when?

BRAD   On the phone.

BRIAN   On the phone when?

BRAD   Twenty minutes ago.

BRIAN   Oh. Oh. Oh.

BRAD   Oh. Oh.

BRAD & BRIAN   Oh.

BRIAN   Well, do you want to come in?

BRAD   Well, that's why I'm here.

> *Sound: Super-sexy à la Barry White.*
> *Light cross fades to deep red.*
> *BRAD seductively takes off his jacket and playfully throws it at*
> *BRIAN. BRIAN catches it. BRAD approaches BRIAN slowly. BRAD*

*loosens BRIAN's collar and tie then puts a hand on his chest walking
him backwards toward the chairs stage right. Just as it seems the men
are about to kiss BRAD drops into the chair and BRIAN slips on the
jacket as he steps to centre.*
Sound: a busy bar.
Light: snaps to PLAY state (two specials).
BRAD becomes PAM ELLIS. BRIAN becomes RAY.

RAY   Ms. Ellis? Pam?

PAM   Pardon me?

RAY   Are you Lloyd's mother?

PAM   Yes.

RAY   I'm Raymond King. Brenda's husband.

PAM   Oh. Yes. Hello. Yes.

RAY   I just wanted to—

PAM   Offer condolences?

　　　　　An uncomfortable beat.

Sorry. It's just that it's different for a woman. I guess. Or maybe not.
How are you?

RAY   Oh there's a lot going on these days. A lot to take my attention.

PAM   That's a good thing.

RAY   That's a good thing.

PAM   I didn't see it coming. Did you?

RAY   I… maybe.

PAM   Or I don't know… maybe I did. It's Lloyd really that I feel worse
for. He'd really warmed to Terry. Since his father left it's been…. But I'll
be fine. It's Lloyd I worry about.

RAY   About Lloyd. I just wanted to let you know I've had my insurance
policy placed in Lloyd's name.

PAM   Oh. You—Oh. Why?

RAY   You never know. Just in case. Accidents happen.

PAM   But why Lloyd.

RAY   Just to say—I'm sorry.

PAM   It's not your fault.

RAY   I'm just sorry that it had to happen.

PAM Yes. Thanks.

RAY Would you tell Lloyd something for me?

PAM Yes?

RAY Tell him the centre of the circle's not so great.

PAM The centre of the circle?

RAY Tell him you can't really see the circle from the centre, and it's all about seeing the circle.

> *A beat.*

PAM You know what my problem is Mr. King?

RAY Ray.

PAM My problem is I'm allergic to loneliness, and as poison as they are to me, men are the only antidote I can find. But sometimes you've got to get sick to get better.

> *RAY laughs.*

Can I buy you a drink Ray?

RAY Sure.

BRAD *(to the audience)* Another drunk woman.

BRIAN Forget about that, what is this?

> *Sound: out.*
> *Light snaps to SHOW state.*
> *BRIAN takes a folded poster from his pocket and holds it up for the audience. The poster is a photograph of BRIAN and BRAD side by side (wearing what they're wearing now). BRAD has his head thrown back laughing, BRIAN looks very uptight.*
> *Note: This moment works best if the image shown is the actual image used in publicity materials for the production.*

What is this?

BRAD The poster for the show.

BRIAN There is no "show."

BRAD There is now.

BRIAN This is not acceptable.

BRAD Why not?

BRIAN Look at it. What's it supposed to be?

BRAD   *(holding the photograph up for the audience)* Well there's me and I'm laughing at something and there's you and you're not getting the joke.

BRIAN   Yes I'm sure everybody's seen it.

BRAD   What's wrong with it?

BRIAN   Look at it. What's it supposed to mean? Look at me! I look like I wouldn't know fun if it bit me.

BRAD   Well if the shoe fits…

BRIAN   Oh that's sweet. And what's so funny anyway?

BRAD   That's the point.

BRIAN   The point is, you make me look terrible.

BRAD   Well what would you like to look like?

BRIAN   Obviously not the way you see me.

BRAD   Oh here we go.

BRIAN   Oh here we go where?

BRAD   The village of image.

BRIAN   Yes well it's my image.

BRAD   Anyways…

> *Light snap to the PAST.*
> *Sound: distant Lesley Gore.*

BRIAN   "Anyway!" "Anyway!" There is no such word as "Anyways!"

BRAD   Don't! Don't correct me!

BRIAN   I'm not it's just…. You use it a thousand times a day. It's driving me to distraction.

BRAD   Anyways! I just wish you could be yourself.

BRIAN   What? What do you mean? What's that supposed to mean?

BRAD   Forget it.

BRIAN   No. What? What do you mean "yourself?" I am myself.

BRAD   Fine.

BRIAN   No. What's myself?

BRAD   Like this ridiculous opera thing. You don't even like opera.

BRIAN   I do so.

BRAD   You like Maria Callas. Maria Callas is not opera. Liking Maria Callas is like liking Barbra Streisand.

A beat.

BRIAN   Take that back.

BRAD   You just think you should like opera because cultured people like opera—you think being an opera buff elevates you from your shameful working class background.

BRIAN   Anything else?

BRAD   You present yourself as this benign... this open minded... guardian of all things tasteful...

BRIAN   When in fact?

BRAD   When in fact you use your opinions—or the opinions you borrow from other people—

BRIAN   Oh!

BRAD   —in order to manipulate the situation to maintain control.

BRIAN   Well. If that's the way you feel...

BRAD   If that's the way I feel what?

BRIAN   Maybe we should just forget it.

BRAD   Forget what?

BRIAN   Nothing.

BRAD   Forget what?

BRIAN   Everything. I don't think we're working. I don't think we care anymore.

BRAD   What are you waiting for?

BRIAN   Exactly.

BRAD   No. What are you waiting for?

BRIAN   For something to happen.

> *Light snap to SHOW state.*
> *BRAD holds up the photograph once again.*

BRAD   That One, the laughing one, represents something happening, and This One, the serious-looking one, represents waiting for something to happen. And it sort of means that, if you don't think about it too much, you'll realize, it's probably already happening.

BRIAN   Okay.

BRAD   Like in this next part.

Sound: a grandfather clock chimes.
Light snaps to PLAY state. (Two specials, BRAD in his, BRIAN just outside.)
BRAD becomes RAY's father, IRVING.

IRVING   Leave me be leave me be I'm not an invalid, I can get around just fine on my own steam thank you very much. Thug.

BRIAN   You don't have to play it like an "old man."

IRVING   I'll play it any way I want to. Thug! I can't find my thingamajig. I've been looking for it everywhere and I can't find it.

BRIAN steps into his light as RAY.

RAY   Your which?

IRVING   My thingamajig—the whatsit with the thing—with the stuff in it. The brown one with the thing. You know.

RAY   No I don't, Dad.

IRVING   The travelling box.

RAY   What?

IRVING   The travelling box. The box for travelling.

RAY   A suitcase?

IRVING   No. Is that?… Oh yes. Is that right? Yes I guess yes, suitcase.

A beat.

My hands are all gone funny.

RAY   What about it?

IRVING   What about what?

RAY   The suitcase.

IRVING   Oh no I didn't bother with it since I couldn't find it. I won't be gone long anyway.

RAY   Where are you going?

IRVING   Nowhere. They've got thugs working here. Thugs. Guns and everything. One of them pulled a knife on me.

RAY   He was handing you a butter knife, Dad. Dad I have to tell you something. You're won't be seeing me again.

IRVING   What's your name?

RAY   Raymond King. Ray.

IRVING   You ever kill a man Ray?

RAY   No.

IRVING   It's quite a thing. Had to of course had to. That was the thing. It was human lives at stake.

RAY   Yes.

IRVING   My uniform's gone. Took that too, the bastards. That was the thing. The uniforms. Because you just didn't think about it and you just put it on and that's what you wore and that's who you were and that was that. And what happened to the trains? They're always driving you around now. I don't like to be driven. But I like the trains. All over Germany that was a lovely train. And Spain.

> *Sound: distant trains.*

Very high-class quality, high-class type surroundings type trains they've got in Spain. But Germany I liked better—because I've got a little Spanish you know, because of my French, I've got a little French and Spanish is pretty close to French. But I haven't got a lick of German. So I preferred that. The German trains. Where I couldn't understand a word. There's nothing better really. On the train and people all around you and you know they're not talking to you—and even if they were all you've got to do is *(shrugs shoulders)* and pretty soon you're left to yourself and the lovely little towns and the countryside changing and changing and the trains and the trains... I keep waiting for something to happen. I keep waiting and waiting for something to happen.

RAY   I know.

> *Sound: little girls playing.*

IRVING   My little skipping girls have all gone home.

RAY   Who?

IRVING   From the lawn. Your mom made cookies but the girls were gone. There's lots left if you want some. Extra raisin kind.

RAY   I better go now Dad.

IRVING   What's your name?

> *RAY looks at IRVING*

RAY   Raymond King.

> *Silence.*
> *BRAD faces BRIAN.*

BRAD   Now what?

BRIAN   Ray leaves his father and he gets into his blue Mercedes.

BRAD   And you'll be Ray?

BRIAN   And I'll be Ray.

BRAD   And I'm me?

BRIAN   Yes.

>   *BRAD and BRIAN step downstage and address the audience. BRIAN becomes RAY.*

You've got to run some errands.

RAY   What it comes down to now is intention.

BRAD   Pick up a prescription for somebody's migraine. Toilet paper. Exchange some tickets. The usual.

RAY   What it comes down to now is the difference between intention and accident.

BRAD   A usual day. Not a bad day just a usual day.

RAY   In my big powerful fast machine.

BRAD   In the car driving along. Aware of the machinery—big powerful fast machines passing a lot of other big powerful fast machines driven by people about whose sobriety nor mental state you know nothing. That thought's a bit too heavy.

RAY   Just another accident.

BRAD   You go for the radio.

RAY   Just like everything.

BRAD   Crap.

RAY   Just like everything.

BRAD   Crap.

RAY   Just like everything.

BRAD   More crap.

RAY   I wish I'd said I'm sorry more.

BRAD   Crap.

RAY   I wish I'd said I know less.

BRAD   Something familiar.

RAY   I wish I never said "nothing" when I meant something.

BRAD   Crap.

RAY   And I'm glad my mother's gone…

BRAD Back to something familiar.

RAY …and that my father won't know the difference.

BRAD Where was it?

RAY And Brenda will sing at my funeral…

BRAD Can't find it.

RAY …and Terry will love her…

BRAD One oh one point what?

RAY …and Lloyd will be fine…

BRAD Or after?

RAY …and Pam is a beautiful woman…

BRAD No before the sports after the metal.

RAY …and Miles is just me but lost sooner.

BRAD There it is.

RAY And just a quick jerk of the wheel.

BRAD And in that moment…

RAY Just like everything else.

BRAD It's the headlights of the blue Mercedes.

RAY Just another accident.

> *RAY closes his eyes, seeing what BRAD is describing.*

BRAD An incredible vortex of slow motion and silence. Spinning through time, lighter than air, weightless. Weightless and perfectly calm. You look out the window and it's filled with sky—the tops of buildings and trees and electrical wires slowly moving past, and as they do they turn to smoke. A thick black smoke that takes a moment to disperse. Everything turns to smoke then holds its shape for a moment then drifts away from itself. The leaves the wires the trees the buildings. And you feel sad that it's going but at the same time you feel this blissful peace at being able to witness it go away. And you think: "This is what it's like to die." But no, then you realize; "No…

> *RAY opens his eyes.*

No, this is what it's like to be alive." And then…

RAY And then you're gone.

BRAD …you're gone.

Light slowly fades to black.
We wait in the blackout for some time as if the play is over. Just before
the audience applauds and in the blackout BRAD speaks.

Do you really find this a satisfying ending?

BRIAN   What?

BRAD   I just think there are probably a few more options.

BRIAN   For God's sake.

BRAD   Do you mind?

BRIAN   Whatever.

Light snaps to PLAY state.
BRAD addresses the audience as he sets the two chairs centre.

BRAD   First date. My idea. We go to a play.

BRIAN   It was hardly a play.

BRAD   It was this performance thing Kate was putting on.

BRIAN   What was that anyway?

BRAD   It was interesting.

BRIAN   Faint praise.

BRAD   But it's this thing where we're supposed to arrive at nine, and we get there and there's nobody else around except the box office guy—so he sells us our tickets and he sends us around the back of the building. This One's already complaining.

BRIAN   I was not, I was on my best behavior.

BRAD   Everything's relative. Anyway. We go in the back door and it's this big empty warehouse space *(Note: here BRAD would briefly describe the set for this production should there be a set.)* and these bright lights.

BRIAN   Blinding.

BRAD   And in the middle of the space there are these two chairs. And I can tell immediately that This One wants to bolt.

BRIAN   But I don't.

BRAD   But he doesn't and we sit in the chairs and nothing's happening and nothing's happening and then we hear somebody laugh. So we look around and about thirty meters out past the lights is the audience of—

BRIAN   Hundreds!

BRAD   Fifty maybe. And you know first it's like "What the hell is going on?" and then it's like "Oh my God they think we're the show!"

BRIAN   Oh my God.

BRAD   And then it got kind of weird because we don't know what to do.

BRIAN   So we just sit there.

BRAD   So we just sit there and pretty soon they're thinking "They don't know what they're doing."

> *A long silence as BRAD and BRIAN find themselves back in the strange, uncomfortable moment. BRAD is loving it, BRIAN is mortified.*

BRIAN   And then it got kind of tense.

BRAD   And then it got kind of nice.

BRIAN   It did?

BRAD   I took your hand.

> *BRAD takes BRIAN's hand.*

BRIAN   Yes you did.

BRAD   Which was like I might as well have kissed him full on the mouth This One is so in the closet.

BRIAN   *(pulling his hand away)* I am not.

BRAD   Anyway.

BRIAN   Anyways.

> *BRIAN puts his hand on BRAD's leg for a moment.*

It was nice. Although once I got to know you I was convinced you just took my hand as one of your radical political statements.

BRAD   *(honestly; looking at BRIAN)* Well I didn't.

> *A beat. BRIAN looks away.*

BRIAN   Well, I guess it's an option for an ending, but it's a bit sentimental.

BRAD   You ain't seen nothing yet. Hit it Kate!

> *Sound: "Sunshine, Lollipops and Rainbows" plays from the top. BRAD grabs the chairs and rushes them back to their opening position. He rushes back and begins the dance. BRIAN is horrified, slowly he joins it until they both dance the ridiculous dance, laughing and loving it.*

The dance ends. BRIAN faces the audience as if to take a bow. BRAD indicates to the audience that it's not over yet. BRIAN looks at BRAD. BRAD moves to step off the stage.

BRIAN   Where are you going?

BRAD   To pick up your prescription.

Light slow fades through SHOW to PAST state, a hybrid. BRIAN pauses until:

BRIAN   Didn't you do that yet?

BRAD   I'm doing it now.

BRIAN   God.

BRAD   What?

BRIAN   Nothing.

BRAD   Good. Do we need anything else?

BRIAN   Yes, toilet paper for the how many-eth time.

BRAD   Right right right.

BRIAN   And could you please exchange those tickets.

BRAD   I'll do it tomorrow.

BRIAN   You said that last week.

BRAD   We've exchanged them three times already.

BRIAN   Fine we'll give them away.

BRAD   Keep a schedule.

BRIAN   I do.

BRAD   Write it down!

BRIAN   I did.

BRAD   Pin the list to your mitten!

BRIAN   Well then don't.

BRAD   No fine fine.

BRIAN   Try Saturday.

BRAD   A change charge and an upgrade?

BRIAN   Fine.

BRAD   Tuesday?

BRIAN   No Kate's bringing Karen over to meet us on Tuesday.

BRAD   We met Karen already.

BRIAN   "Privately."

BRAD   Great.

BRIAN   She's your friend.

BRAD   What's that supposed to mean?

BRIAN   She doesn't call me any more.

BRAD   You can't pick up the phone?

BRIAN   Why is it always my fault? Why is everything always my fault.

BRAD   We have to talk.

BRIAN   I have a migraine.

BRAD   You always have a migraine.

BRIAN   We'll talk when you get back.

BRAD   Fine.

BRIAN   Try Wednesday.

BRAD   Wednesday.

BRIAN & BRAD   Next Wednesday.

BRIAN   And shampoo.

BRAD   And shampoo.

> *BRAD moves to leave again.*

BRIAN   How are you getting there?

BRAD   I'm riding my bike.

BRIAN   To the mall?

BRAD   Sure.

BRIAN   And the theatre?

BRAD   Yeah.

BRIAN   You're not going to go to the theatre if you take your bicycle.

BRAD   I need the exercise.

BRIAN   I just want to get this dealt with.

BRAD   I'm dealing with it.

BRIAN   Here it's going to rain anyway, take my car.

BRIAN reaches into his pocket and mimes throwing keys to BRAD.
BRAD pretends to catch the keys he has been hiding in his hand.
BRAD moves to step off the stage. He turns back.

Prescription, toilet paper, tickets and?...

BRIAN   You've helped me to see the beauty in people and you've been a really good friend.

BRAD   *(mildly scolding)* That's not how it went.

BRIAN   Shampoo.

BRAD   Shampoo.

BRAD steps off the stage and walks through the audience toward the door of the theatre.

BRIAN   And not the cheap shit.

BRAD   Right right.

BRIAN moves to centre.
Light slowly fades down to special on BRIAN as at top of play.
BRAD exits the theatre slamming the door.
Sound: footsteps on a gravel driveway, a car door opening, a car door shutting, a car start, a car pull out of the driveway, driving, driving, driving. BRIAN speaks against the sound.

BRIAN   Of course another option would be... for an ending... would be to take it all full circle. To end up back where we began. People like a package. People like a tidy package. So.... So.... Ray leaves his father and he gets in his car and instead he goes back to the Doctor. And Ray says: "Hey Doc." And the Doctor says: "How are you Ray." And.... And then Ray says: "How long have I got Doc." No let's give him a name. Charlie. And Ray says: "How long have I got Charlie." And the Doctor says: "I can't answer that question Ray." And Ray says.... Ray says: "Come on Charlie we've got the verdict what's the sentence."

Sound: driving, driving, driving.

And the Doctor says: "I can't—" and Ray interrupts him and he says: "I need a number Charlie a number." And the Doctor says: "Well at this point it could happen at any time. We could be talking about days or weeks. Maybe months. Possibly as long as thirty or forty years. But the bottom line is each day could potentially be your last and so I would advise you to start living your life accordingly." And then a look of confusion, which slowly becomes understanding then relief. Ray looks out at the audience—almost smiling but still unsure. Then he steps off the stage, through the audience, out the door, into the world ready to begin his new life.

Sound: A signal light. A radio turned on, bad music, news, sports, bad music, the Maria Callas aria, news, a search to find the aria again, finally finding the aria. A long sustained note over tires squealing. A huge explosive impact. Accident scene sounds. Female voices shrieking: "Oh my God! What happened?" "The blue Mercedes swerved right into him." etc. Sirens. Police band radio. Finally the aria alone.
BRIAN takes off the jacket and holds it. He waits for the final phrase and completion of the aria. It stops in a pause, not finishing.
BRIAN holds the jacket out before him.

But why are we talking about endings anyway. Some things end. But some things just stop.

BRIAN drops the jacket on the floor where he picked it up at the top of the show. BRIAN turns and leaves the stage. Just as he disappears from view the aria finishes.
Light fades to spot on jacket then black with end of aria.
End.

For Paul Bettis

A Beautiful View

l to r: Caroline Gillis, Tracy Wright
photo by Kevin Fitzsimons

A Beautiful View was developed by da da kamera in workshop in Toronto, Ontario with VideoCabaret and in Montreal, Quebec with Playwrights Workshop Montreal and in Residency at Usine C, Montreal and co-produced and premiered by the Wexner Center at Ohio State University, in February 2006, with the following company:

L . . . . Tracy Wright
M . . . . Caroline Gillis

Directed by Daniel MacIvor
Assistant Director and Lighting Designer: Kimberly Purtell
Sound Designer: Michael Laird
Produced by Sherrie Johnson
Production Assistants: Eric Colleary (Wexner),
    Daniel Arnold and Medina Hahn (Toronto and Montreal)
Assistant to Daniel MacIvor: Brad Horvath

•

Thanks to Daniel Brooks, Tucker Finn, Arlea Ashcroft and Shrimp.
The lyrics of the song "Four In MY Ever" are written by Tucker Finn. Tucker Finn can be reached through <tuckerfinn.com>.

•

This project is made possible in part by a grant from the Association of Performing Arts Presenters Ensemble Theatre Collaboration Grant Program, a component of the Doris Duke Charitable Foundation Theatre Initiative.

Characters

L: a woman in her 30s – 40s
M: a woman in her 30s – 40s

Note

The characters are called L and M. The actresses choose their own names. In the original production Tracy Wright chose Liz and Caroline Gillis chose Mitch.

A Beautiful View

Prologue

Lights, general. A state called SHOW.
A boom box on stage playing sounds of the woods at night, crickets,
wind through the trees, an owl, a loon.
A woman, L, enters and regards the audience, then the boom box, then
the audience. She leaves.
Another woman, M, enters, looks with concern toward the lights
overhead. A loon on the boom box, she steps toward the boom box and
regards it, waiting for the loon again, it never returns.
L enters with a chair. She sets it facing toward M and leaves.
L returns with another chair. She sets it facing the first chair. Then
sits in the first. M regards the chairs, then returns her attention to the
boom box.
L rises and moves the second chair a few feet further away.
M regards this change and then sits. M turns the chair slightly
upstage facing the boom box.
After a moment L rises and turns off the boom box. She returns to her
seat.
A moment of silence.

LIZ   Maybe we should start?

MITCH   Not yet.

LIZ   When?

> *A moment.*

MITCH   What's it going to change?

LIZ   Everything maybe.

MITCH   Or nothing.

LIZ   "Nothing is enough."

MITCH   Yeah.

> *A moment.*

LIZ   I'm sorry.

MITCH   Yeah.

LIZ   Nothing is enough.

> *M takes a quick look at the lights then away.*

Don't be scared.

MITCH   I'm not scared.

LIZ   You've always been scared.

> *A moment.*

They're going to wonder if you don't like me.

MITCH   Why?

LIZ   Sitting like that.

MITCH   It's not about you.

LIZ   Yeah yeah.

MITCH   Okay whatever.

> *M turns to face L.*

Go ahead.

LIZ   What do you see?

MITCH   What do you see?

LIZ   My best self.

MITCH   Ha.

LIZ   What do you see?

MITCH   Nothing.

LIZ   Oh.

> *A moment.*

MITCH   Nothing is enough.

LIZ   Ha.

> *A moment.*

We should start.

MITCH   From where?

LIZ   From the beginning.

MITCH   *(looking toward the audience)* It's bright.

LIZ   Look under the light.

> *M does so.*

MITCH   Oh God. They're beautiful.

> *M rises, holds her hands out at the audience, looking at them, smiling.*
> *L comes and stands beside M looking out as well. L waves.*
> *Blackout.*

Scene 1

M carries on a two-person tent. She opens the back and crosses through it into the scene.
M and L stand facing out, addressing one another through the audience.

LIZ   Excuse me?

MITCH   Hi.

LIZ   I'm looking for a job.

MITCH   Oh yeah?

LIZ   I heard you were hiring?

MITCH   Oh—

LIZ   Who should I talk to?

MITCH   Someone who works here?

LIZ   Oh. Sorry.

MITCH   Don't be sorry. I could work here. I wouldn't mind working here.

LIZ   It's just that I saw you coming out of the tent.

MITCH   Yeah. I was lying down in it. They say you should always lie down in a tent before you buy it.

LIZ   I've heard that.

MITCH   You a camper?

LIZ   Yeah, it's great to, you know, get out of the city.

MITCH   Yeah yeah.

LIZ   Get away.

MITCH   Live, be, breathe, let go.

LIZ   Yeah.

MITCH   Yeah. These days I'm working full time on some live, be, breathe, let go.

LIZ   How does that pay?

MITCH   Or whatever yeah.

LIZ   No I mean yeah.

A moment.

You're not working?

MITCH   No like you.

LIZ   Well, now I work in a bar but I'd rather anything else.

MITCH   Which bar?

LIZ   Oh, not, airport.

MITCH   Bartending?

LIZ   Yeah.

MITCH   I'd love to be a bartender.

LIZ   Yeah.

MITCH   Bartending's cool.

LIZ   It's not so, it's all right. Are you looking?

MITCH   No I'm, busy with my band.

LIZ   You've got a band?

MITCH   Yeah, we're just—under the radar. For now. Intentionally.
Ukeular. Two girls with ukuleles. The girls sing. Occasionally a bass.
Guitar. Drummer. We cover 80s tunes.

LIZ   You sing?

MITCH   Drummer.

LIZ   I play guitar.

MITCH   Really? Wanna be in my band?

LIZ   Um. Don't you already have a guitar player?

MITCH   No yeah right.

LIZ   So?…

MITCH   Yeah.

LIZ   You have a camping trip planned?

MITCH   I was thinking about up north.

LIZ   But did you read about—

MITCH   Yeah yeah.

LIZ   Did you see that this morning?

MITCH   Well it happened last week.

LIZ   Right right, but it was on the news this morning.

MITCH   How insane.

LIZ   Totally. Mauled and eaten.

MITCH   They were smearing—Did you read?

LIZ   I know, peanut butter.

MITCH   —on their hands—

LIZ   Hello!

MITCH   —to attract bears!

LIZ   Bears!

MITCH   Bears!

LIZ   People are idiots.

MITCH   People get what they deserve.

> *A moment.*

LIZ   You a big camper?

MITCH   Getting back into it. Used to. Like three years ago. I was a different person then, a different species.

LIZ   Right.

MITCH   Anyway.

LIZ   I'll keep an eye out for your band.

MITCH   Yeah yeah. We'll be out there.

LIZ   Ukelear?

MITCH   Ukeular.
Right.

> *L walks away.*

Happy camping.

LIZ   You too.

MITCH   Hey.

> *L stops and turns back.*
> *Light shift to SHOW.*

That's not fair.

LIZ   In what way?

MITCH   In what I end up looking like.

LIZ   Is that what you're worried about?

MITCH   That is so…

LIZ   At least we establish that we're both liars.

MITCH   Whatever.

> *M picks up the tent and departs.*
> *L regards the audience briefly and departs in the opposite direction.*
> *L returns with a boom box.*
> *She turns on music. A live band.*
> *L stands and watches out as if listening to the music live.*
> *M enters and stands watching the band as well.*
> *Light shift.*

Scene 2

> *M and L both enjoy the band.*
> *M notices L as if across a crowded dancefloor.*
> *M recognizes her.*
> *After considering it, M approaches L.*
> *L continues to enjoy the band.*
> *M moves as if she is struggling through a crowd gathered at the front of the stage at a gig. Apologies. Spilled drinks. Rudeness.*
> *M finally reaches L as the song ends.*

MITCH   *(cheering)* Whoohoo. *(to L)* Hi.

LIZ   Hi.

MITCH   Hi. Remember me? We met at Outdoor Outfitters? The Girl in The Tent?

LIZ   Oh yeah hey hi.

MITCH   Hi.

> *The band begins its next song. A moment.*
> *L and M speak over the music.*

LIZ   *(re: band)* They're great eh?

MITCH   Yeah.

> *A moment.*

So do you really play guitar?

LIZ   You mean was I lying?

MITCH   No I mean like, are you good?

LIZ   I'm okay.

MITCH   No I just, in case I lost my guitar player or something.

LIZ   You must know lots of guitar players.

MITCH   No yeah but no yeah.

LIZ   Because I'm not so good.

> *A moment.*

MITCH   They're great eh?

LIZ   Are you friends with them?

MITCH   The band?

LIZ   Is it a different scene from your band?

MITCH   No, yeah, no. I know the drummer.

LIZ   Sasha?

MITCH   Yeah.

LIZ   She's great. How do you know her?

MITCH   I'm a drummer. Drummers know drummers.

LIZ   Is she still with Kevin?

MITCH   Kevin?

LIZ   Yeah.

MITCH   Yeah.

LIZ   Really?

MITCH   No.

LIZ   No?

MITCH   On and off.

LIZ   Yeah yeah.

> *A moment. L moves to depart.*

Gotta pee.

> *L picks up the boom box and departs.*

MITCH   Well maybe I'll see you at the airport sometime.

LIZ   Right on.

MITCH   If I'm ever going away. Or coming back.

> *Light shift to SHOW.*

(to the audience) Okay so now I have to go to the airport. Because I lied. I mean I don't know the drummer. But that's not the big lie. That's just conversation. I mean I knew the drummer, she was the drummer, I mean I knew who she was, which is like... you know? But who's Kevin? I thought the drummer was a lesbian. Anyway I didn't know the drummer but I knew who she was.

A moment.

And I didn't have a band. I once worked in a record store. There was a lot of talk about the band. But I didn't really know any musicians, just other people like me who worked at record stores and talked about starting a band. And I was really close to thinking about learning the drums. And I thought it was a really good idea. Specifically Pat Benetar covers. And this was some time ago—and I mean even now it could work. With the right... tone. It was a good idea. So it wasn't really a lie, it was just wishful thinking.

A moment.

But the lie was about Sasha and Kevin, "Off an on?" I didn't even know Sasha and who was Kevin? So for the sake of Sasha and Kevin I had to go to the airport.

Scene 3

L enters carrying two cocktail menus.

LIZ   For one?

MITCH   Hi.

LIZ   Oh hi.

MITCH   From the—

LIZ   No yeah no, hi.

MITCH   You're hard to find.

LIZ   Sorry?

MITCH   There are a lot of bars in the airport.

LIZ   Nervous people like to drink.

M laughs.

MITCH   This is the nicest, one, bar in the airport.

LIZ   Where are you headed?

MITCH   What?

LIZ   Or are you coming back?

MITCH   I'm picking up my grandma.

LIZ   What flight is she on?

MITCH   Mid-nightish.

LIZ   Halifax?

MITCH   Hey. Yeah.

LIZ   Eleven-fifty.

MITCH   Right. Actually that's not true.

LIZ   Yes, no, yes, I think they might have changed the time recently, Halifax used to come in at 11:40 but they moved it, which I don't know exactly how that benefits—

MITCH   No I mean I'm not picking up my Grandma. She's not coming here. Actually she's dead. But she was from Halifax though.

LIZ   Oh.

> *A moment.*

Could you excuse me a second?

MITCH   Sure.

> *L turns her head and looks at the audience.*
> *Light shift.*

LIZ   *(to the audience)* Okay so, it's eleven-thirty on a Saturday night. I'm minutes from getting off work. I'm working at some weird combination of a shopping mall and the army. At this moment the place is filled with a bunch of drunk Cape Bretoners waiting for their relatives and composing dirty sea shanties. It's the kind of thing you really need a few beers to enjoy. And I'm working. And all of a sudden the weird girl from the camping store is standing in front of me telling me her grandma's dead. So what's she doing at the airport? And I'm afraid to ask because I'm afraid that she's going to say she just came out for a drink. All the way from downtown, to the airport, for a drink? And so she's trying to pick me up. Big deal. Not my thing. But you know, who cares? I'm off people generally, not even hiring in the friend department. Plus I once had a guy I met at a play who came out to the airport "for a drink" and that was a bit strange. And anyway I don't know for sure that she's a lesbian.

> *L turns back to M, light shift.*

Sorry.

MITCH   No problem. I came out this afternoon but you weren't here.

> *L turns to the audience and gives them a knowing look. L turns back to M.*

LIZ   So did you just come out for a drink?

MITCH   I don't know Sasha, I don't know why I said that, I mean I know who she is, I see her around but I don't know her, and I don't know if she and Kevin are off or on or whatever, and so I didn't want you to tell Sasha that somebody said they were on and off in case they were very on and then she thinks that's Kevin's line that he uses, and then Kevin's screwed, probably through no fault of his own.

LIZ You know Kevin?

MITCH No I don't know anybody. And I don't have a band but I'm thinking about getting one going.

LIZ Oh.

MITCH So. Anyway.

LIZ Would you like a table?

MITCH You're not bartending tonight?

> *L looks out at the audience.*
> *Light shift.*

LIZ *(to the audience)* And some people just remind you of things. Things that have happened. Things about yourself. It's nice to have someone around to remind you.

> *L looks back at M.*
> *Light shift.*

Oh, no I, no, I just, I say I'm a bartender but really I'm a hostess.

MITCH Oh.

LIZ Well at least we've established that we're both liars.

MITCH I like to think of it as wishful thinking.

LIZ Will you have a drink?

> *M looks at audience. Light shift.*

MITCH And I think, oh my God, she's a lesbian.

> *M looks back at L. Light shift.*

I could have a drink.

> *Light shift to SHOW.*
> *M exits.*

LIZ *(to the audience)* I've always considered myself a practical person. And maybe we're born practical. Babies are very practical. All that screaming is very practical. We mistake those screams for feelings. But they are not. Feelings develop because needs aren't met. Feelings are not practical. I don't mean feelings like, I like this song or this pie is delicious or this bath is relaxing or this bitch is dead. That's pretty practical. In my case I was born practical and remained practical out of necessity. My parents were insanely impractical. My mother was a chronic alcoholic and my father left when I was four—which I guess when you consider it might have been very practical, for him. By the time I was 7, I had learned the numbers for Yellow Cab, Chickees Ribs And Wings We Deliver and Goldman Locksmiths. That's a practical kid. I've always been drawn to practical things. Like camping. Camping is very practical. How you pick a site, the best time to arrive, planning meals, organizing hikes. You rise with the sun you sleep with the moon. All very practical. Of course there are the odd impractical things like mosquitos or poison ivy. Or bears. Especially bears. They say there are ways to avoid a bear attack. But sometimes.... There's something about bears. If I could physically manifest fear it would take the form of a bear.

> *M enters with a large plastic fig tree.*

MITCH   Nerd.

LIZ   Feelings are like bears. They follow their own rules. And as difficult as it might be sometimes you just have to not be practical and have a feeling.

MITCH   Are you talking about me?

LIZ   No. *(re: tree)* Is that plastic?

MITCH   It doesn't matter.

LIZ   Is it necessary?

MITCH   I like it.

LIZ   Fine.

Scene 4

LIZ & MITCH   *(to the audience)* And so we have a drink at the airport.

> *Through the following L and M go and get the chairs and place them facing one another. L gets the boom box and places it upstage.*

LIZ   I get off work.

MITCH   I have two glasses of wine.

LIZ   I have a few beer.

MITCH   *(to L)* "A few?"

LIZ   Four's a few.

MITCH   "Four?"

LIZ   And we have all this weird stuff in common.

MITCH   We both have the same birthday.

LIZ   *(to M)* Do you know anyone else with the same birthday?

MITCH   *(to L)* Just you.

LIZ   I know. Me neither. Just Martin Landau, and I don't even know Martin Landau.

MITCH   And neither of us can swim.

LIZ   And we're both terrified of bears.

MITCH   Which we find hilarious.

LIZ   Even now.

MITCH   And she says "If fear had four legs it would be a bear."

LIZ   Something like that.

MITCH   *(to L)* Nerd.

LIZ   *(to M)* Nerd? Prophet.
     I leave my car at the airport.

MITCH   We take a cab downtown.

LIZ   Everything's closed.

MITCH   And we're having fun.

LIZ   I know a place.

MITCH   *(to L)* That place is awful.

LIZ   But she doesn't want to go.

          M sits.

MITCH   And she says, do you want to come to my place for a drink?

LIZ   And she says yes.

          L turns on the boom box. A song plays under the scene.
          Light shift.

MITCH   Nothing is enough.

          L steps toward M in the chair.

LIZ   What?

MITCH   "Nothing is enough." On your fridge. At the top of that bunch of words. By the picture of the girl.

LIZ   That's Sasha. The picture.

MITCH   Oh.

L sits.

LIZ   I don't really know her that well. I just like the picture.

MITCH   I'm sorry about—

LIZ   Oh whatever. So you like "nothing is enough?"

MITCH   Yeah. Do you mean it the good way or the bad way.

LIZ   The good way definitely.

MITCH   Me too. I mean I'm searching.

LIZ   Searching?

MITCH   I mean everybody's searching.

LIZ   Everybody's searching.

MITCH   I mean are we going to go there? Are we getting into the "God" thing?

LIZ   What the hell.

MITCH   Because—

LIZ   But I've got to say the whole religion thing—

MITCH   The "religion" thing, God! Yeah yeah exactly.

LIZ   Of course on paper though. A lot of it works on paper.

MITCH   Sure sure.

LIZ   Everything works on paper.

MITCH   Everything works on paper.

LIZ   Fascism works on paper.

MITCH   Yeah.

LIZ   Satanism works on paper.

MITCH   Really?

LIZ   Sure. Everything works on paper. But just add humans.

MITCH   Exactly exactly.

LIZ   And it's all about shutting up.

MITCH   It's all about shutting up.

LIZ   Blah-de-blah-de-blah.

MITCH   Blah blah blah.

LIZ   Shut up!

MITCH   Yes yes. Now the Buddhists have—

LIZ   Oh they have all that chanting.

MITCH   Yes the chanting.

LIZ   Fuck chanting.

> *M laughs with guilty delight.*

Just silence.

MITCH   Silence. Yes.

> *During the following the song on the boom box stops.*

LIZ   And the silence is there, underneath all the blah-de-blah. But nobody can hear it. Silence is God. Silence is God saying "Shhh." But nobody can hear it. And even if they could hear it they'd be too busy listening for something to hear it. We'll never hear anything until we shut up and stop listening for something so hard we can't hear it.

MITCH   Whoa.

LIZ   You know?

MITCH   Yeah yeah.

> *A moment.*

LIZ   Here's to shutting up.

> *A moment.*

MITCH   Here's to shutting up.

> *A moment.*

Because, how do you mean "Nothing is Enough," like do you mean "Nothing is sufficient," which I kind of think is the good way, even though I mean, there's like "Nothing will ever be enough," which is not really bad, but different. Or does it matter?

> *L shrugs.*

Anyway.

> *A moment.*

I love your place.

> *L shrugs.*

That's one sick fig.

> *L shrugs.*

(finding the idea weird and delightful) Should we not talk?

L shrugs.
M is silent. She finds it weird and delightful.
The silence reaches another level.
And another.
The women are about to kiss.
M rises quickly. Light shift to SHOW.

And that's why I wanted the plant to be here. It's not a real fig, and it's not sick—well it's not sick because it's plastic, but it was important to have it represented, because of what it represents. Because in that moment of "that's one sick fig," it seems like I was seeing the healthy fig that I would have had. Just because I said the fig was sick didn't mean I meant she was cruel or heartless or maliciously trying to kill the fig. That's just what came out, it was just something to say. And I think that's interesting because some people say that there's a lot of truth in that stuff that just comes out, but sometimes we're just looking for something to say. And I just think that's funny.

LIZ   I think it's funny that you stopped right there.

MITCH   Stopped right where?

LIZ   Stopped where you stopped.

MITCH   When?

LIZ   Just now.

> *L rises.*

MITCH   Well it was pretty obvious where it was headed. *(to the audience)* It was pretty obvious, it's not like we have to—

LIZ   It's pretty funny.

MITCH   You know what I think is pretty funny?

LIZ   "Garfield?"

> *Through the following L takes her chair, M's chair and the plant offstage.*

MITCH   I think it's pretty funny that you had a picture of Sasha on your fridge but you didn't know her.

LIZ   It was a flyer for some gig.

MITCH   That's pretty funny.

LIZ   The first time I really talked to her was at that art show with the "box of light." I so don't get art.

MITCH   Anyway.

LIZ   But what's really pretty funny is that you stopped right there, where you stopped, to talk about the plant. Especially since you stopped to say that what you said about the plant didn't mean anything. That's a little funny don't you think?

MITCH   A little odd, maybe.

LIZ   Kind of like you were just looking for something to say.

> *A silence.*

Do you remember what happened then?

MITCH   The music started again all by itself.

> *Music on the boom box.*
> *They slowly begin to dance together to the music. Light shifts through. M begins to unbutton her shirt. L helps her. M takes off her shirt. L takes it from her and drops it on the floor.*
> *They stop dancing and stand close.*
> *L picks up the boom box and motions for M to follow her offstage. They depart.*
> *Blackout.*
> *In the dark we hear M return to the stage. The lights come up catching M looking for her shirt. As she speaks to the audience she puts her shirt back on.*

(to the audience; whispering so as not to wake L) Which is also really funny, really odd, the music starting again all by itself. Which seemed like it was a sign. The music was a sign that I should, you know, let go, for a second, for a minute, for a night. And so, well, I did and it was... I mean, I wasn't thinking about it, it just was, and it was.... But then when I did think about it later on, at four in the morning, I just couldn't. I mean. I couldn't go getting bisexual on myself. I mean that might work for some people but trust me I do not have the constitution for it... I mean the thing is you have to be very organized to be a bisexual and and I am in no way an organized person. So, due to that, and due to just, my things, the next morning I quietly, quickly disappeared.

> *Blackout as M departs.*
> *A flashlight cuts the darkness on stage. L enters wearing a fleece jacket, carrying a flashlight. Lights up. L steps forward to address the audience.*

Scene 5

Light shift to SHOW.

LIZ   Time passes. And I keep thinking about that crazy lesbian who I met at Outdoor Outfitters and who performed this elaborate seduction and we had a great night together and then she evaporates. And I just think, okay so crazy lesbians are just like men. A year passes. My mother dies. Which was hard, but time passes. I move a couple of times. I "change careers," several times. I re-meet a guy I used to know. We have some good laughs. There's no stress. We get married. Because that seemed like the thing to do. I mean, he's a good guy. He likes camping. Good laughs. No stress. We go camping quite a bit. This one weekend I go camping.

M enters wearing a fleece and carrying the tent. She almost hits L with the tent.

Whoa!

M places it down between she and L.

MITCH   Oh sorry. Is this a path?

LIZ   Hi.

MITCH   Hello. I was trying to get something near the bathrooms but it was jammed. It's getting dark isn't it? What time does it get dark?

L doesn't say anything. She illuminates her own face with her flashlight.

(recognizing her) Oh my God. Oh hi. Hello. Hi.

LIZ   Hi.

MITCH   You're camping?

LIZ   Yeah I started again.

MITCH   Me too. Where's your spot?

LIZ   By the bathrooms.

MITCH   Lucky you.

A moment.

LIZ   Are you by yourself?

MITCH   Is it dangerous?

LIZ   No no, not at all.
Hey Sasha and Kevin split up.

MITCH   I didn't know them.

LIZ   Right.

MITCH   I was lying.

LIZ   Right lying. Or what did you call it.... "Wishful thinking."

MITCH   Yeah.

> *A moment.*

Are you alone?

LIZ   No my husband's at the site.

MITCH   Your husband?

LIZ   Yeah.

MITCH   A man?

LIZ   Well yeah. Why?

MITCH   Oh no, just, how's that working out?

LIZ   Good.

MITCH   Have you switched over entirely?

LIZ   To what?

MITCH   ...Men?

LIZ   I never left. Well I mean, there was you.

MITCH   What do you mean? There was more than me.

LIZ   No.

MITCH   I thought you were a lesbian.

LIZ   No. Does that matter?

MITCH   Well. No.

LIZ   Do you only sleep with other lesbians?

MITCH   I'm not a lesbian.

> *A moment.*
> *They consider this.*

That's funny.

LIZ   Or sad.

MITCH   Yeah.

LIZ   *(heading off)* Maybe I'll see you tomorrow.

MITCH   Yeah.

L stops.

LIZ   What are you doing for dinner?

MITCH   There's a place up the highway.

LIZ   Join us.

M shrugs.

Come on.

MITCH   Okay thanks.

LIZ   Bring your flashlight.

It is night now L and M turn on their flashlights and light one another.

(to M) And you come for dinner.

MITCH   *(to L)* That was really nice of you.

LIZ   *(to the audience)* And we have some food.

MITCH   The food was excellent. And smores!

LIZ   And we have some drinks. Too much to drink.

MITCH   *(to L)* And I meet your husband.

LIZ   *(to M)* And you don't like him.

MITCH   *(to L)* No I do.

M and L step together they are lit by flashlights and the orange glow of a campfire.

LIZ   *(to M)* No you don't.

MITCH   No I didn't.

A moment. They speak to one another only now.

It's not that he was a bad guy.

LIZ   We had some laughs.

MITCH   "Good laughs. No stress."

LIZ   Exactly.

MITCH   But when the laughter goes away there's nothing left. Sometimes the stress holds up the laughter.

LIZ   Maybe.

MITCH   I don't think he really cared, about anything.

LIZ   Maybe I didn't care.

MITCH   You cared.

LIZ   Oh shut up.

> *A moment.*

He was good to have camping.

MITCH   He was damn good to have camping.

LIZ   Thanks.

> *Light shift to SHOW.*

Scene 6

> *M steps forward to address the audience taking off her fleece.*
> *L removes the tent.*

MITCH   Life happens. We become friends. I'd never been in therapy. She's been in and out for years. It wasn't for me. But she convinces me to go. To hers. But we think maybe that's not allowed or something by the rules of whatever. So I start going to him too but we don't tell him. That we're friends. But we always talk afterward and compare notes. It happened you know, organically. But which is for sure not allowed. And he had this style. This don't-say-anything style. Which was kind of driving us both nuts. So she decided.

LIZ   *(off)* You decided.

MITCH   We decided that she'd just never say anything either, and I'd just never stop talking. To see if one of them would make him say something. So this goes on for like, months. Me just yapping from the moment I walk in the door to the moment I leave and she's like *(zips and locks her lips and throws away the key, calling off)* Was it a year?

> *L crosses and takes M's fleece and flashlight.*

LIZ   Nine months.

MITCH   And one night we're out having dinner at this fancy place for some occasion.

> *L crosses off.*

LIZ   My divorce.

MITCH   Oh my God, yeah. And he walks in.

LIZ   *(exiting; to the audience)* The therapist.

MITCH   With this woman.

LIZ   *(popping back on for a moment)* Not his wife.

MITCH   *(to L)* You don't know that.

LIZ   *(to the audience)* Not his wife.

     L exits.

MITCH   And that was something, but the really something was when he saw us. Her and me, the silent one and the mouth, sitting together.

LIZ   *(off)* Flipped a nut.

MITCH   They had to lock him up.

     L re-enters with two ukuleles.

LIZ   He took a break.

MITCH   He quit.

LIZ   He opened up a B and B.

MITCH   And there we were, suddenly out of therapy.

     L hands a ukulele to M.

LIZ   So we started a band.

     Light shift.
     L and M play and sing Pat Benetar's "Heartbreaker" with a full recorded backing band for a gig. They stop suddenly.

MITCH   That was our first gig.

     M takes the ukuleles offstage.

LIZ   It was at a party.

MITCH   At an art show.

LIZ   It was more of a party than an art show.

MITCH   *(off)* We felt pretty good about it.

LIZ   All you cared about was what Sasha thought.

MITCH   That's not true.

LIZ   Oh yeah?

MITCH   Not "all" I cared about.

LIZ   Oh yeah?

Scene 7

     Light shift.
     A box of light on the floor.

MITCH   What did Sasha think? What did Sasha think?

LIZ   About what?

MITCH   Ukular?

LIZ   She said it was fun.

MITCH   That's all she said? "Fun."

LIZ   She liked it.

MITCH   You were talking to her for a while.

> *L looks at box of light on floor, up into source.*

LIZ   What's this?

MITCH   "Box of Light."

LIZ   "Box of Light."

MITCH   Yeah.

LIZ   What does it do?

MITCH   I think it just is.

LIZ   I so don't get art.

MITCH   So what else did Sasha say?

LIZ   *(looking off)* Oh my God look at Norman. The work he's had done! He's calling that a peel. That's some peel. What were they trying, to peel him back to 1974?

> *A moment.*

MITCH   What did Sasha think of the band?

LIZ   She said it was fun. She said it was ironic.

MITCH   Ironic.

LIZ   Ironic in a fun way.

MITCH   You mean the name? She thought the name was ironic? Should we change it?

LIZ   The name is fun. It's your name. It's your band.

MITCH   It's our band. Did she think I played okay? I played so bad.

LIZ   Well it's not a guitar or something.

MITCH   What?

LIZ   It's hard to play a ukulele badly, it's not like it's a guitar.

MITCH   Is that what Sasha said?

LIZ   She said something about a guitar.

MITCH   What about a guitar?

LIZ   That it's not really a band without a guitar.

MITCH   Should we have a guitar?

LIZ   It's called Ukular.

MITCH   I know.

LIZ   You don't get the same bang from "Guitar-ular."

MITCH   She thought we were terrible.

LIZ   No.

MITCH   She thought I was terrible.

LIZ   No. She said you had a lot of personality.

MITCH   "Personality." What's "personality?" That sounds like something that wears on people. That sounds like something that people get tired of.

LIZ   It's fun.

MITCH   I want it to be more than fun.

LIZ   What's more than fun?

MITCH   I want it to be for real.

LIZ   "For real"'s not fun?

MITCH   What else did she say?

LIZ   She wanted to know who seduced who.

MITCH   Of whom?

LIZ   Me and you.

MITCH   She knows about that?

LIZ   A few people know about that.

MITCH   How?

LIZ   I mentioned it to Norman at the time.

MITCH   Oh no.

LIZ   Don't worry. He's sworn to silence now.

   A moment.

MITCH   What did you say?

LIZ   About what?

MITCH   Of who and whom.

LIZ   I said I didn't know. But she made a guess.

MITCH   Who did she guess?

LIZ   She guessed me.

> *M looks at the box, up into the source. Steps into the box. M looks up into the source, eyes closed.*

Does it say to do this anywhere?

MITCH   No.

LIZ   Wow. Are my feet still on the ground?

MITCH   Yeah.

LIZ   Wow. This is good. Try this.

> *L steps into the box of light and mimics M's stance. (The size of the box allows them to stand facing, a foot between them.)*

What do you feel?

MITCH   Nothing.

LIZ   *(happily)* Yeah me too.

> *A moment.*

Uklear.

MITCH   Ukular.

LIZ   Yeah.

MITCH   What do you think?

LIZ   It's fun.

MITCH   It's ironic. In a good way.

LIZ   Yeah.

> *A moment.*

MITCH   You're really good.

LIZ   I'm not sure I want to do the band thing for real.

MITCH   You have talent.

LIZ   No I don't.

MITCH   Yes you do.

LIZ   Talent is need. I don't need it.

MITCH   You want to quit?

LIZ   No, just not do it for real, just for fun.

MITCH   You're really good.

LIZ   I think you need to need it, I don't need it.

MITCH   I think I might.

LIZ   Then you should.

MITCH   I think I want to learn the guitar.

LIZ   Then you should.

MITCH   Will you teach me?

LIZ   Yeah.

>   *Light shift.*
>   *L departs.*
>   *Light shift to SHOW.*

Scene 8

>   *M approaches the audience.*

MITCH   Let me tell you a little something about learning to play the guitar. It's hard. And it hurts. I mean your hands aren't made to… *(calling off)* And how old were we then?

LIZ   *(off)* Twenties, late twenties.

MITCH   No. Thirties. Early thirties. Whatever. But let me tell you a little something about learning to play the guitar. Start'em young. It's such joy. But it wants those fresh muscles and bones. Anybody here has a kid, knows a kid, next birthday give them a guitar and some lessons. If even one person here tonight does that my life will have meant something.

>   *L enters with a guitar and holds it out for M.*

You're not serious.

LIZ   Come on.

MITCH   I can't play the guitar.

LIZ   Yes you can.

>   *M takes the guitar from L. She puts it on. She considers it a moment.*

MITCH   Not in front of people.

>   *M exits with the guitar.*
>   *L steps forward to address the audience.*

LIZ   Time passes. Things happen. Men appear. Men disappear. She has a semi-serious thing with a dentist and I keep thinking about my ex. Every couple of months my ex calls about getting back together. And I think "why not?" So we meet up for a… drink. And then I know why not. Her dentist thing ends badly. She gets a cat. Who apparently defines cat-ness.

MITCH   *(off)* I have pictures.

LIZ   She has pictures.

MITCH   *(entering)* So?

>   *M takes up a position addressing the audience.*

Time passes.

LIZ   I move a lot. She moves a lot. I move more.

MITCH   Summers and summers and springs and falls.

>   *Light shift.*

LIZ   Christmas 2000.

MITCH   Not the next year.

LIZ   Not the next year.

MITCH   You went home.

MITCH & LIZ   And one, two, three more.

LIZ   Five summers and winters and springs and falls. And hundreds of mornings and midnights and thousands of long lunches.

MITCH   Hundreds of thousands of lunches.

LIZ   A number of trips.

MITCH   And quite a bit of unemployment, and three record stores, some temping, and two weeks in a swanky restaurant oh my God, three forks, please, and a tiny inheritance, and I wrote something once for a thing, and a few gigs that paid, and a ton that didn't.

LIZ   And some plays and stuff.

MITCH   She's been in movies.

LIZ   *(reassuring audience)* You haven't seen them.

MITCH   And a really bad fight.

LIZ   And a really bad fight.

>   *Light shift.*

Take responsibility! Things don't just happen. It's not about other people. And stop caring what other people think! Other people only think about themselves, if they think about you it's only in relation to themselves! It's just a way to take it off yourself! You take it off yourself and leave it all to me! Stop expecting me to be the strong one! I'm not strong! For once I'd just like you to take responsibility!

> *Light shift.*

Sorry.

MITCH   No. You were right.

LIZ   At least we talked.

MITCH   At least we talked.

LIZ   And lots of laughs.

MITCH   And I got Dixie.

LIZ   And she got Dixie.

MITCH   I have pictures.

LIZ   And lots of laughs.

MITCH & LIZ   Lots and lots of laughs.

LIZ   And a healthy amount of stress.

MITCH & LIZ   And let's get out of here. And how's your drink? And let's go dancing. And you look hot! And I'm on fire. And get off your ass. And it's only early. Life's too short. Let's have fun.

MITCH   And how many hangovers?

LIZ   How many Sundays?

MITCH   How many Wednesdays?

MITCH & LIZ   And a bowling league.

MITCH   I met the dentist.

LIZ   She got a trophy.

MITCH   I'm good to bowl.

LIZ   And how many bands?

MITCH   And Kurt Cobain.

LIZ   And Kurt.

> *Music: a simple line from Nirvana's "All Apologies" drifts through space and is gone.*

MITCH   *(sadly)* Ahh.

LIZ   And how many bands.

MITCH & LIZ   And Chan and Sarah and Jann and Joni. And Superchunk, and Superfriends, and Sloan and The Hip and The Truth and The Treeo. *(They hoot.)*

LIZ   And Ukular.

MITCH   We only played once.

LIZ   We never stopped. We're the band!

MITCH   The band has left the building.

LIZ   And lots of laughs.

MITCH   And the Halloween party.

LIZ   Really?

MITCH   That's why we're here.

LIZ   That's why we're here.

> *A moment.*

Put on some music.

MITCH   We have to go.

> *Light fade to black as M and L depart.*

Scene 9

> *Sound: A cat meows.*
> *L enters putting on a tie.*

MITCH   *(off, calling for Dixie the cat)* Dixie-dixie-dixie-dixie-dixie.

LIZ   Maybe you should just leave the door open.

MITCH   *(off)* I'm part of the incentive. *(calling for the cat)* Dixie-dixie-dixie.

LIZ   The incentive to what?

MITCH   *(off)* What?

LIZ   The incentive for Dixie to do what?

MITCH   *(off)* To come in.

LIZ   Maybe you should try a saucer of milk.

MITCH   *(off)* Ha ha. Dixie.

LIZ   I think you'd get farther with saucer of milk.

MITCH   *(off)* I can see her. Dixie!

LIZ   Try a saucer of milk.

> *M enters wearing an* Anne of Green Gables *hat and pigtails.*

MITCH   So what do you think?

LIZ   Cute.

MITCH   So you're going as Norman?

LIZ   Yeah.

MITCH   For Halloween?

LIZ   Why not?

MITCH   How long did it take you to think of that?

LIZ   About a minute. Are you Pippi Longstocking?

MITCH   No.

LIZ   Dorothy.

MITCH   I'm Anne Shirley of course.

LIZ   The orphan? Didn't she have curly hair.

MITCH   No! Not Annie, Anne. "Oh Ma'am, I'm not troublesome, I'm just some trouble." From *Green Gables*?

LIZ   Oh yeah. I was more Nancy Drew.

MITCH   Do you give Dixie milk when you cat sit?

LIZ   What?

MITCH   Do you give Dixie milk when you cat sit?

LIZ   No.

MITCH   Because she's totally laxtose intolerant.

LIZ   "Lactose."

MITCH   What?

LIZ   Nothing.

MITCH   Do you give her milk?

LIZ   No. Sometimes ice cream.

MITCH   Ice cream?

LIZ   The yogourt kind. Once.

MITCH   It would make her sick.

LIZ   That's a great costume.

MITCH   It's just a hat.

>   *Sound: A cat meows.*

(looking off) There you are.

>   *M exits.*

(off) Did you miss Mommy? Did you miss Mommy?

LIZ   Is everybody really getting dressed up?

MITCH   *(off)* It's Halloween.

LIZ   Maybe I should think of something else.

>   *M enters.*

MITCH   No, Norman will love it.
You don't even know who Anne of Green Gables is do you?

LIZ   Yes. There's books. It's a musical.

MITCH   Have you seen it?

LIZ   No.

>   *Sound: A cat meows.*

MITCH   *(calling off)* Hi there honey. Hi there honey. Come see Auntie. Auntie's here. Come see Auntie. Come on honey. Come on honey. Come see Auntie. Come see Auntie.

LIZ   That's okay. *(waving off to the cat)* How ya doin.

>   *L moves off.*

MITCH   And that's good enough for you, "How ya doin."?

LIZ   *(off)* Yeah that's good enough for me.

MITCH   We are so different.

LIZ   *(off)* Is that bad?

MITCH   No.

>   *L returns with a beer.*
>   *L and M stand side by side looking out. Light shift, night on a porch.*
>   *They share the beer.*

I have to work tomorrow.

LIZ   How's that going?

MITCH   It's weird. Typical temp. It's an office.

LIZ   It's on what like the hundredth floor or something?

MITCH   Something like that.

LIZ   I'll give you a month.

MITCH   I miss cigarettes.

LIZ   Sometimes.

MITCH   Why did we quit?

LIZ   Because we want to live forever?

MITCH   Do we?

LIZ   I don't know.

MITCH   What do you suppose happens?

LIZ   When?

MITCH   After?

LIZ   After what?

MITCH   Later. After we... you know.

LIZ   Die?

MITCH   Yeah.

LIZ   We go to a place where we're standing on the edge of a cliff. Looking out over an endless landscape of ancient pristine redwoods and low rolling hills lined with stands of birch. And in the middle is a river that rushes to a split. And one arm runs to a lake surrounded by green clearings and elm trees, and the other arm runs to a waterfall that crashes down into a freshwater pond where no one has ever been. And then we're there, the first person ever there, and we turn and see someone, and we look into their eyes and we see all of our history. Something about ourselves, something good about ourselves. Our best self.

MITCH   Do you think?

LIZ   Not really.

MITCH   What do you really think happens?

LIZ   Nothing.

MITCH   Nothing?

LIZ   Pretty much.

>   *A moment.*

MITCH   But nothing is enough though. Right?

LIZ   I guess.

A moment.

We're like a couple aren't we?

MITCH   A couple of what?

LIZ   What are you afraid of?

MITCH   That everyone's going to think I'm Dorothy.

L steps away.

Scene 10

M moves forward to address the audience.

MITCH   And it's Halloween and I'm Anne Shirley and she's Norman and we're going to a party. And there's a lot of people there.

LIZ   There's lots of people there, people I don't know.

MITCH   She's looking for Norman.

LIZ   Not everybody knows Norman so when people ask me who I'm supposed to be most people think it's just a dumb costume. So I'm looking for Norman.

MITCH   I get a lot of comments on the hat, everybody gets that I'm Anne.

LIZ   Sasha thought you were Dorothy too.

MITCH   Sasha's at the party.

LIZ   Sasha's at the party.

MITCH   I never really liked Sasha, once I got to know her. She thought I had a lot of personality.

LIZ   You do.

MITCH   Uh huh. And people drink. There's some food. That goes fast. A few people dance. But then the neighbour complains about the music being too loud, and it's hard to dance if the music's not too loud. And so people mainly drink. So I decide to go around and make sure no one's driving. And I realize I haven't seen her in ages. But I haven't spent much time in the kitchen, so I go into the kitchen, but she's not there.

LIZ   I'm upstairs.

MITCH   With Sasha.

LIZ   With Sasha.

MITCH   And they're not just talking.

LIZ   We ended up having sex.

MITCH   "Ended up?" Whatever. And I walk in.

>   *Light to M alone through.*

It's dark but I can make out two people on the bed. One of them is Sasha and the other one is her. Her hair is a mess and her shirt is pulled way up. And all I can think to say is: "Pull your shirt down I can see your nipples."

>   *Light shift to L.*

LIZ   What are you doing in here? Get out. Get out. Get out.

>   *Light restore.*

MITCH   *(to L)* "What are you doing in here get out?"

LIZ   I was drunk.

MITCH   That's not an excuse.

LIZ   No.

>   *M takes off the hat and moves to leave, she stops.*

MITCH   And I maintain that if she thought about me for one second, just one second, me, it wouldn't have happened.

LIZ   Why were you so upset? Because it was Sasha?

MITCH   Because it was you.

>   *Light fades to black*
>   *Light restores. L and M haven't moved.*
>   *M exits.*

LIZ   Time passes. After that night, we don't speak. I try to but she won't. And there was so much to say and nothing at all to say. Like time. Time can pass so quickly and—

>   *M enters with the guitar. L stops talking.*
>   *M plays the guitar and sings a song she wrote. (In the first production the song was written by Tucker Finn of the Jane Waynes.)*

MITCH   *(sings)* I'm bitter I'm jaded
I don't trust my own mother
To love me and stand by my side
I shacked up with lovers of all shapes and sizes
And repeatedly love crashed and died
So when I say what I say oh please don't take it lightly
Because I can't believe that it's true
I'd packed up my bags to move to a planet

Where love couldn't break me in two
I tested the waters with one little toe
Now I'm ready to make a big splash
If I had to gamble my heart on one person
I know where I'd lay down my cash
Because you're the one in my only
The two in my gether
and if there is such a thing
you're the four in my ever.

> *L leaves.*

(continuing) I'm tired and cranky
I don't care for people
Who don't ever say what they mean
I've wasted my money on psychics and shrinks
Who don't know the places I've been
So when I say what I say
Ne prends pas ça au léger
That's the same line but in French
I'd taken a beating in the game they call love
And I was happy to sit on the bench.

> *L enters in her fleece, carrying a flashlight. M stops playing.*

LIZ   I'm glad you came.

> *M leaves with the guitar.*

I had to stop calling. It was getting weird. You never called back.

> *M is offstage and does not respond. L looks to the audience for a moment.*

Are you still working at that place on the 74th floor or whatever?

> *M enters in her fleece, carrying a flashlight.*

Scene 11

> *Light shift.*

MITCH   Fifty-one.

LIZ   That's like, for a year? So that's going well.

MITCH   The people are nice.

> *A moment.*

I heard there were bears. In the vicinity.

LIZ Where'd you hear that?

MITCH At the office. Checking in.

LIZ They always say that. I think they have to say that. Legally or something.

MITCH You've never seen any bears here?

LIZ No.

MITCH And you've been here before?

LIZ Yeah.

> *A moment.*

Have you eaten?

MITCH I grabbed something on the highway.

LIZ I tried to save the site beside me. But it got late.

MITCH It took me longer than I thought.

LIZ Where'd you pitch bitch?

> *A moment. M smiles but does not laugh.*

MITCH By the bathrooms.

> *A moment.*

LIZ I'm glad you're here.

> *A moment.*

MITCH How was Christmas?

LIZ Good. Low key. Tons of snow.

> *A moment.*

How was yours?

MITCH Odd. My mom died.

LIZ Oh my God, I never even knew that.

MITCH I didn't get into it with many people. I'm with my sisters on the phone a lot. It's okay.

LIZ Oh I'm sorry.

MITCH No it was good. It was all good.

> *A moment.*
> *L looks at the sky.*

LIZ There's lots of stars tonight.

A moment.

Of course there's lots of stars, we're in the woods. Why the hell did I say that, I have no idea why I said that. Stuff people say.

A moment.

MITCH   Here's to shutting up.

LIZ   Nothing is enough.

A moment.

Actually I had always thought of it the bad way. Nothing will ever do. I like it better the other way. Upon considering it. I like it better your way. Nothing is sufficient.

MITCH   It's become all a bit "here's to shutting up" to me.

A moment.

LIZ   Are you totally stuffed because I haven't eaten.

MITCH   No I'm fine. I'm tired. I'll see you tomorrow.

LIZ   There a hike apparently, across two rivers.

MITCH   I'll probably head out after breakfast.

LIZ   Really?

MITCH   Just because, you know. I have nothing to say.

LIZ   But—

MITCH   It's not petty, I heard you said it was petty.

LIZ   That I?

MITCH   Someone said you thought that. It's not petty. Not to me.

LIZ   I know.

A moment.

Why didn't you say anything?

MITCH   What did you want me to say?

LIZ   Whatever you were thinking?

MITCH   What did you want me to think?

LIZ   "I wonder if she's lonely"?

A moment.

MITCH   I'll see ya.

LIZ   See ya.

Light shift as M steps offstage.
L stands silently.
Light shift.
L steps forward and addresses the audience.

And there was so much to say and nothing at all to say. It amazes me how that can be true. Just like time can pass so quickly and so slowly depending on your perspective. Days fly by until you know there's only one moment left—seconds become hours with that kind of information—knowing it's the end.

A moment.

I guess finally for me it's—I mean she says teach your kids to play guitar—I'd say, if I had to say something—and since I can, I'd have to say stop naming things. "I am a," "We are a," "She is a." If we could only let it be what it is and be okay with that. "A friendship." "A love affair." "A soulmate." Those are just names so other people can feel comfortable. It's not about other people. Or maybe... I guess for me it was about her, at this point anyway. And the funny thing was, the odd thing—it was fear that brought us back together finally, in that—

M enters with the boom box. L stops talking. M sets it down between them.

Scene 12

(The following italicized text in all of Scene 12 plays as recorded dialogue. Stage directions are in parentheses for this scene.)

MITCH   *I know I'm such a baby but—*

LIZ   *No no.*

MITCH   *I totally thought I heard something by my tent.*

LIZ   *No no, I mean there's nothing to worry about, I mean bears want to be around people, there are no bears around here.*

(The dialogue continues on the boom box as M leaves and returns with the tent, she sets it and leaves. She returns with a chair, then another, and sets them as L did at the beginning. M sits. L leaves. After a moment she returns with the plant, she sets it beside the tent and then sits.)

MITCH   *They were talking about it at the check-in.*

LIZ   *There's too many people around.*

MITCH   *My side's pretty empty.*

LIZ   This side ain't. Why do people have to bring their kids camping.

MITCH   What are they supposed to do with them?

LIZ   I don't know, Disneyworld.

MITCH   Kids like camping. I liked camping.

LIZ   Yeah.

MITCH   Do you still think people are idiots? That's what you always said.

LIZ   I didn't always say it.

MITCH   Yes you did, you used to all the time.

LIZ   You know what you said once.

MITCH   What?

LIZ   People get what they deserve.

MITCH   I don't think that.

LIZ   You said it.

MITCH   When?

LIZ   Once.

MITCH   Well, once.

LIZ   That's the kind of thing you only have to say once.

MITCH   Well I don't think that.

LIZ   I guess when I say people are idiots I'm thinking more of myself. Hopefully I'm not the only one.

MITCH   Wishful thinking.

LIZ   Yeah.

(Silence.)

We could always just blame Sasha.

MITCH   If that works for you.

LIZ   Why did you not say anything?

MITCH   I did say something.

LIZ   What?

MITCH   "I can see your nipples."

(L finds this hilarious. We hear her laugh for some time. M can't help but join her. They stop and are quiet.)

LIZ   Listen to this.

(We hear L strumming on a guitar.
L sings and plays M's song. After a few moments L joins in.
Underneath this we hear the sounds of a large animal approaching
distantly through the woods. After a time the women hear this, they
stop singing and playing.)

MITCH   What was that?

LIZ   That was something.

    (They grow quiet.)

MITCH   What was it?

LIZ   I think it might be that fat guy a couple of sites over, he came by this afternoon.

MITCH   That didn't sound like—listen.

    (We hear what might be an animal approaching, not close.)

LIZ   We should go to the office.

MITCH   I think we should go to the office.

LIZ   Or what if it's...?

MITCH   What?

LIZ   No we'll go to the office, grab a chair.

    (We hear the tent open and the women leave the tent.)

MITCH   Grab a chair?

LIZ   To walk with, just in case, to make yourself look bigger.

MITCH   Right right. And make noise.

LIZ   And make noise. *(alarmed)* Grab a chair, grab a chair!

    (Blackout.
    The bear growls ferociously.)

Epilogue

Light up. Sitting in their chairs. M faces out, L watches M.

MITCH   What do you see?

LIZ   What do you see?

MITCH   An endless landscape of ancient pristine redwoods and...

LIZ   And low rolling hills lined with stands...

MITCH   Stands of birch.

LIZ   And in the middle is?

MITCH   A river.

LIZ   That rushes to a split.

MITCH   And one arm runs to...

LIZ   A lake surrounded by green clearings and?...

MITCH   Elm trees. And...

LIZ   And the other arm runs to a waterfall that crashes down into a freshwater pond where no one has ever been.

MITCH   And then we're there, the first people ever there.

> *M looks at L.*

And history.

> *L looks out.*

LIZ   Something about myself, something good about myself.

> *L looks at M.*

MITCH   My best self.

> *Fade to blackout.*
> *End.*

photo by Guntar Kravis

Daniel MacIvor was Founder and Artistic Director of Toronto's ground-breaking theatre company da da kamera from 1986 to 2007 and he is one of Canada's most prolific and influential post-modern playwrights. His other plays include *Somewhere I Have Never Travelled, Yes I Am And Who Are You?, See Bob Run, Wild Abandon, This Is A Play, 2-2-Tango, How It Works* and *Marion Bridge.* He is the recipient of many awards including the Village Voice Obie Award, The Edinburgh Fringe First, the GLAAD Award, and the Chalmers New Canadian Play Award.

With long time collaborator Daniel Brooks he has created *The Lorca Play* and the solo performances *House, Monster, Here Lies Henry* and *Cul-de-sac* which have toured throughout Canada, the U.S., Europe, Israel and Australia. Also a filmmaker Daniel's credits include writing the screenplay adaptation of his play *Marion Bridge,* co-writing "Whole New Thing" and writing and directing "Past Perfect" and "Wilby Wonderful." As an actor Daniel has appeared in his own films, "Thom Fitzgerald's Beefcake", Don McKellar's "Twitch City" and Jeremy Podeswa's "The Five Senses."

Daniel's work continues to be produced, published and presented extensively around the world, making Daniel one of the most distinctive and influential artistic voices to emerge from Canada.